WHY?

Interesting Stories, Fun Facts, Questions & Answers about Science, History, Pop Culture, Traditions and More

RIDDLELAND

INTRODUCTION

> "If I had an hour to solve a problem and my life depended on the solution, I would spend the first fifty-five minutes determining the proper question to ask, for once I know the proper question, I could solve the problem in less than five minutes."
>
> -Albert Einstein (1879-1955)

Albert Einstein is credited with saying that if you want to find out information, you must first ask a question. Well, I have some questions:

Why do doughnuts have holes in them? Is it to rip off consumers?

Why are there 24 hours in a day? Why not 25 hours? While we're at it, why are there 60 minutes in an hour? Why not 100 minutes? Were these just arbitrary numbers, and, if so, who picked them?

Why do fortune cookies always get it right? Are they really magic? I don't think they are, but how do they do it?

And excuse me for asking, but why do boogers stick to the wall? Is snot some kind of glue?

Getting a question from one's head onto paper is not easy. I admit that I have had lots of great ideas for songs, books, and business plans flow through my head - and that's where they have stayed. I suspect that from time to time you too have asked similar questions to the ones I asked above, but you may not have been able to put the question into words or on paper. If you didn't, don't worry, by the time you are done reading this book you will likely know the answers to your questions and, more importantly, you will likely have lots of "why?" questions of your own.

This is a book of "Why?" It answers questions about time and space, daily life, food, health, technology, and even gross stuff like boogers. Each question can stand alone, so feel free to read the questions that interest you the most first and come back to the other questions later. As I wrote the book, I tried to answer a question a day; that gave me time to ponder about the answer - but you can move at whatever pace you want.

You and I are going to be lifelong learners. A lot of the things that we are learning in school will be out of date in a few years, so, we not only have to learn about how life is today, but we must also learn how to learn so we can be our own teachers after we graduate from school. To be our own teacher, we must be able to phrase questions and we must dare to answer them; two things this book encourages. I think Albert would be proud of both of us!

TABLE OF CONTENTS

PART I

TIME AND SPACE

CHAPTER 1

Why Are There 24 Hours in a Day?

Did you use your fingers when you learned to count? If you did, you probably used your left hand to count 1-5 and your right hand to count 6-10. If you were trying to count higher than ten, you probably joked that you needed to take off your shoes and socks so you could count to 20.

Boys and girls growing up in ancient Egypt learned to count with their hands too, but they counted to twelve on a single hand. Hold your hand out and let me show you how. Notice that you have four fingers, and each one has three places where it bends. Touch your thumb to the underside of the tip of the pointer. That is "one." Pull the thumb below the first joint; that is "two." Move it down below the next joint; that is "three." The children would count 1-3 on the pointer finger. The second figure had numbers 4-6, the ring finger had 7-9, and the pinky had 10-12. When they ran out of fingers, they would start over, just like when we use up all our fingers we say "ten plus one" or eleven. They had a base twelve counting system; we have a base ten.

A day consisted of the sun coming up and the day going down in ancient Egypt, just as it does for us today; to be more scientific, a day is the period of time it takes for the earth to make one revolution on its axis. Whereas we grew up with base ten and like to cut things in tenths, the ancient Egyptians grew up with base 12, and so they liked to cut things in 12ths - so they divided the day into twelfths and the night into twelfths, and they created a sundial so they could see which 12th they were currently in.

Not everything ran smoothly for the Egyptian astronomers and clockmakers. Although a day is always a day – the earth makes a complete revolution on its axis every 24 hours, an hour of daylight is not always an hour of daylight. If you'll recall, some days are longer than others – June 21 has more daylight than any other day and December 21 has the least amount of daylight; in parts of the year an hour (a 1/12th of the day's light) would go by quickly and in other parts of the year it would drag. To accommodate for the variance, Egyptians later said a day had twelve hours, but that two of those hours were a blending of light and darkness; they allowed an hour of twilight at sunrise and an hour of twilight at sunset.

Sundials do not work at night, but Egyptians kept track of night hours as well. To track nights, they used the stars. The astronomers observed that the same constellations came up year-round to mark an hour, but just as days were longer and shorter at different times of the year; at different times of the year these constellations were seen in a more rapid succession than at other points of the year. About 1000 years after the Egyptians invented the sundial, Greeks astronomers announced that hours were going to be standardized by using the Babylonian counting system of base 60; that is, there was going to be sixty minutes to an hour. The concept of hours being fixed, though, did not catch on until around 1300 when mechanical clocks began to be invented.

Fun Facts

The forerunner of the sundial was a wooden post put into the ground; people would judge the time of day based on where the shadows of the post fell.

The first sundial was invented in Egypt around 1500 B.C.E.

The sundial has the least amount of shadow on it at high noon.

Chapter 2

Why Are There 60 Minutes in an Hour?

What is the smallest number that can be divided by 1, 2, 3, 4, 5, and 6?

If you said, "60", you were correct. Sixty is five 12s. In the last chapter, we talked about how ancient people used their fingers to count to twelve. If one had five 12s, one for each finger and thumb, one had reached a milestone. To the ancients, then, 60 was a very important number. (We tend to celebrate 50 for the same reason; it is five groups of ten. Our society makes a big deal out of the fiftieth wedding anniversary, a business being established for fifty years, or someone turning fifty years old.)

Sixty, then, represented a cycle. Therefore, an hour, which was one cycle, was divided into sixty minutes. Prior to this time, hours varied in length, depending on the time of the year. Now, though, an hour had a fixed structure, and it was the same every day. (For some professions, such as academics and sailing, this division into minutes was very helpful. The average person didn't have a time-keeping device, though, so the concept of an hour being sixty minutes was more theoretical than practical.)

The concept of a clock face changed the world of sailing. Have you ever said, "look over there at three o'clock," meaning to look to your right? Today's military does that, and so did the ancient sailors. Ancient sailors would use the clock face to help explain the angle their boat was taking.

People quickly realized, though, that it was not specific enough. For instance, a sailor who set a course for between seven and eight minutes, had a lot of space between the two and could end up literally miles from the desired destination Therefore, each minute was also chopped into 60 pieces. The original minute was called the "prime minute" and the division of it into sixty parts was called the "second minute." In those days, people would say that it was "five prime minutes and two second minutes;" today, we would say it is five minutes and two seconds.

Ever wonder why the circle on a clock face has sixty minutes, but a circle in geometry is 360 degrees? It is because the clock is built around a day and a compass is built around a year. Sumerian and Babylonian astronomers arrived at the 360 by looking at the moon and concluded there were 360 days to a year. Because the earth took 360 days to make a circle, when it came to setting up geometry, the ancients declared that a circle has 360 degrees.

The moon also determined the length of a week. Astronomers noticed that a moon phase lasted for seven days. Therefore, astronomers determined that there were seven days to a week.

Fun Facts

Sumer and Babylonia were located in what is known as Iraq and Iran today.

The days of the week are named after heavenly bodies: Sunday (sun); Monday (moon); Tuesday (Mars); Wednesday (Mercury); Thursday (Jupiter); Friday (Venus); and Saturday (Saturn). These were the only large, heavenly objects the Babylonian scientists could see.

Every degree has a spot on the clock. For instance, 90 degrees is three o'clock and 360 degrees is twelve o'clock.

Chapter 3

Why Do Clock Faces with Roman Numerals Often Have a "IIII" for "4" Instead of "IV"?

Do you chuckle to yourself when you see a mistake made by a professional, such as seeing a spelling error on a sign or a proofreading error in a book? Do you wonder why nobody caught the error? Did it make you feel good to find the error, and yet sad that the professionals hadn't seen it?

The other day I was looking at a clock. Although our society does not use Roman numerals a lot, we still use them sometimes; for instance, we use them for designating Super Bowls and on many clock faces. This particular clock had Roman numerals, but instead of having "IV" for 4, it had "IIII".

Now, I know my Roman numerals, and I assume you do too. For those that don't, here is a quick history of why they look the way they do:

One is written as "I;" it is symbolic of holding one finger in the air or putting one tally mark on a log.

Two is written as "II;" it is symbolic of holding two fingers in the air or putting two tally marks on a log.

Three is written as "III;" it is symbolic of holding three fingers in the air or putting three tally marks on a log.

Five is written as "V;" it is symbolic of the forefinger and the thumb being shown to indicate the hand was full.

Four is written as "IV;" that is, one before V, meaning that one is subtracted from five. It's not standard form, but four can also be written as "IIII" to symbolize four fingers in the air. Because "IV" was an abbreviation for the god Jupiter, some Romans were uncomfortable using it as a symbol for four.

Six is written as "VI;" that is, one after V; meaning that one is added to the five.

Seven is written as "VII;" that is, two after V, meaning that two are added to the five.

Eight is written as "VIII;" that is, three after V, meaning that three are added to the five.

Ten is written as "X;" it is symbolic of having the two thumbs cross over each other to show that both hands are full.

When I saw the "IIII" I figured somebody at the factory didn't realize the proper way to write a four in Roman numerals was "IV." When I pointed out the error, I was told that indeed "IV" is the correct symbol for four, but that this error was intentional. It was made because many people get "IV" and "VI" confused, but they clearly know that "IIII" is four. The error was also made because "IIII" is much more pleasing to the eye than "IV."

Fun Facts

The Ivy League began with four schools- Princeton, Yale, and Harvard and either Columbia or Dartmouth. It called itself The League of Four and wrote its name as The League of IV. People began to pronounce the "IV" as "I.V.;" " I.V. " was soon corrupted into "Ivy."

Roman numerals do not have a symbol of zero.

The largest symbol in Roman numerals is M for 1,000.

The highest one can count in Roman numerals is 3,999; that is MMMCMXCIX.

Chapter 4

Why Does the Calendar Have Twelve Months?

Did you realize that there are ten years in a decade, that there are 10 decades in a century, and that there are ten centuries in a millennium? Wouldn't it make sense, then, to have a year be made up of ten months instead of twelve?

It certainly would, and believe it or not, there used to be ten months to a year. If you look closely at the name of the months, you'll recognize prefaces that give away this little-known fact. For instance, October features the preface "Oct" which means eight; for instance, an octagon is an 8-sided figure. October used to be the eighth month. Another easy to recognize one is the preface "Dec" in December. "Dec" means ten, such as in the word "decade." December used to be the tenth month of the year.

The early calendar consisted of ten months, that is, ten moon cycles. It began with the month of March and went through December. Early farmers used the calendar to help them plant, grow, and harvest their crops. Nobody kept track of days during the winter months.

Roman Emperor Julius Caesar wanted to change that. He added January and February to the calendar so that it could be used year-round. January was named after the Roman god Janus, a two-faced human-like figure which symbolized new beginnings. January 1 was declared the start of a new year, and we still celebrate New Year's Day to ceremoniously welcome a new year.

February became a catch-all month. For the calendar to work, the days on the calendar had to equal the days required for the earth to complete a trip around the sun (or, as they thought in those days, for the sun to complete a trip around the earth.) They needed to add in 28 days to accomplish this. As time went by, they noticed that the calendar was outpacing the sun. To correct this, they added extra days one year to allow the sun to catch up. They eventually realized another ¼ was needed each year; therefore, every fourth February has 29 days.

Julius Caesar was so endeared by the Romans that when he died, they changed the month of Quintilis, meaning fifth month, to July in 44 B.C.E. Meanwhile, the sixth month, known as Sextilis, was renamed August in 8 B.C.E. in honor of his successor, Caesar Augustus. Both of these months were extremely important to Roman patriots, and therefore both were given 31 days.

In October 1582, Pope Gregory XIII locked in the calendar as we know it. Some people still use the Julian calendar, and some turn to Jewish, Islamic, Chinese, or Hindu calendars, but, on the whole, the world conducts business under the twelve-month calendar. In fact, it has become such a staple of society that most people don't even consider the prospect that other calendars even exist.

Fun Facts

The month of March is named after the Roman god of war, Mars. March was the first month of the Roman calendar, and its name signified that war was about to resume.

June is named for Juno, the Roman goddess of youth.

The Romans considered May to be a summer month.

Chapter 5

Why Can't We See the Sun at Night?

Before I answer this question, I want you to do me a favor. Find a lamp and go stand by it. Do you see the lamp as you stand there? Now, turn to the right until your back is facing the lamp. Do you see the lamp now? Next, keep turning until you come full circle. Now, do you see the lamp? Go ahead and make a second turn slowly and notice how the lamp will gradually exit your view and then be seen again by you as you spin back around.

The process you just did with the lamp is essentially the same process the earth does with the sun. Although from our perspective it appears that the sun sets in the west and rises in the east, in reality the sun never moves from its central location. Instead, the earth moves. As the earth moves eastward, it appears that the sun, which is staying in place, is moving westward.

When you had your back to the lamp, you could no longer see the lamp, but another part of you was facing the lamp. That is what happens with the earth too. While it is night in half the world, the other half is experiencing day. The earth rotates, so it is always day somewhere and night somewhere else.

It doesn't feel like we are moving, does it? That's because we cannot feel this speed. When we as humans sense that something is moving fast, it is because we are able to compare it to something else. Because everything around us is moving at the exact same speed – our school building, our tree, and the girl standing in the lunch line – we cannot sense that it is moving. If something moves, such as the girl in the lunch line taking a few steps forward, we can tell she moved because we can compare where she was to where she is.

Do you recall how you saw a piece of the lamp come into view as you spun around and then saw it all, and, as you started to spin? Because the world is spinning east, the sun will gradually come into view; we interpret this as the sunrise. As the earth is gradually moving westward, the sun will be leaving our vision, and therefore it appears to set in the west.

Fun Facts

People at the equator where the earth is the widest are moving at about 1,000 miles (16,000 kilometers) per hour.

Sunlight is white. (Sunlight appears yellow from our perspective on earth because the whiteness mixes with water that is in the air.)

Sunsets after a rainstorm appear brighter than normal sunsets. (This is because the rain has washed down pollution that was in the air.)

Chapter 6

Why is January 1st Celebrated as New Year's Day in Western Culture?

Can you imagine celebrating New Year's Day on any day but January 1? To those of us who have grown up with January 1 as the date for a new year, celebrating on January 1 makes perfect sense. Ask someone to specify why we celebrate New Year's Day on that day, though, and you will probably be told because the earth completed another lap around the sun. While that is true the exact same case can be moved from for other days; for instance, why not celebrate New Year's Day as February 12 each year, for the earth will have completed a lap around the sun since the previous February 12. I wasn't satisfied with the general answer, and so I began a quest to find why that specific day was chosen. Here is what I discovered:

People in the West generally choose January 1 as the start of a new year. The Roman calendar originally had ten months that covered the growing and harvest season, spanning the months of March to December. When Roman Emperor Julius Caesar made the calendar into a year-round phenomenon, he added the winter months January and February to open the year. The Roman calendar was later adopted and slightly modified by Pope Gregory XIII, and then it was spread throughout both civil and religious Western Society.

That's why we in the West believe January 1 is New Year's Day. As global celebrations of New Year's Day become more common, the rest of the world appears to be gravitating to it. However, unbelievably, many Eastern societies start the New Year at different points of the year. These are based on past calendar traditions, the moon, the sun, or the weather. For instance,

- The Christian Orthodox societies celebrate New Year's Day on January 14; they still follow the Julian calendar.

- The Chinese celebrate it based on the movement of the sun; it varies, falling between January 21 and February 20.

- The Persian New Year begins at the March equinox, March 20 or 21.

- The Islamic New Year begins with the sighting of the moon July 31 or August 1.

- The Coptic New Year used to begin in mid-July when the Nile River flooded.

- The Jewish New Year begins the seventh month of the Jewish calendar, typically between September and October.

- The ancient Celtic people celebrated it on November 1; this was a harvest festival marking the completion of one cycle.

- The ancient Greeks celebrated the New Year at the winter solstice, the shortest day of the year, December 21.

Many people from these groups follow the Gregorian calendar for their daily lives but still keep their traditions alive by celebrating the New Year on their calendar.

Regardless of one's culture, New Year's Day is typically celebrated as a time to make a new start. (Did you make any resolutions last New Year's Day?) To inspire each other, we frequently clink glasses. It is also a time to scare away evil spirits that might harm us; hence the Chinese shoot off firecrackers; early American colonists shot off guns; and today we typically blow noisemakers and shoot fireworks.

Fun Facts

46 B.C.E. is the longest year in history; for the Julian calendar to get in sync with the earth's rotation, Julius Caesar had to add 90 days to that year.

Right before midnight on New Year's Eve, Spaniards eat a dozen grapes, one for each month of the upcoming year.

Because the earth is rotating around the sun, different countries experience the New Year of January 1 at different times; the first country to experience a New Year is the island nation of Kiribati which is right across the International Date Line.

PARK 2

HOLIDAYS
AND
CUSTOMS

Chapter 7
Why Do We Clink Glasses After a New Year's Toast?

Here is a fun experiment to try outside with your friends. Take a full glass of water and add food coloring to it. Give each of your friends a glass of water too but leave their glasses clear. Next, make a toast, such as, "To interesting tales from history," and clink your glasses together. Watch how their drinks become the color of your drink.

You may think that kings, chieftains, and other rulers had it easy in the past compared to the peasants they ruled, but being a leader meant having a lot of enemies and having a lot of people who wanted your position of power. One way to assassinate a ruler was by poisoning the ruler. To counter this, rulers had food tasters. However, assassins were tricky, and some could bypass the food taster, so rulers took extra steps of caution.

Rulers often traveled to meet with their peers in the other person's kingdom. For instance, the French ruler might travel to England. Being surrounded by people one didn't trust and already being paranoid about what one ate led rulers to be even more cautious about eating and drinking than normal. Therefore, when the time came for the rulers to gather to toast, each ruler made sure that the contents of his beverage ended up in everybody else's beverage and then watched to make sure that the others drank at the same time he did.

A person might not be able to taste poison, but most people could taste if a wine was good wine or bad wine – and in the 1600s bad wine was everywhere. The term "toasting" came about because in the 1600s a piece of toast began to be placed in the bottom of the wine glass to absorb the acidity of the poor-quality wines.

Because today's wine and champagne are better quality, toast is no longer put in the bottom of glasses. Also, because glasses could crack or break – and because you trust the people you are with, people do not normally smash their glasses together as hard as they did in past days. We still, though, call the clinking of glasses to signal agreement a New Year's toast.

FUN FACTS

The host of a party is expected to make the first toast.

Toasting is more about the friendship than about the beverage, and people can toast with nonalcoholic beverages and/or alcoholic ones.

Attila the Hun likely created the ritual of toasting.

Chapter 8

Why Do People Want to Know If a Groundhog Saw its Shadow on February 2?

Can animals predict the weather? If a frog croaks louder than usual, is a storm coming? If dogs are acting funny, is it going to rain? If a groundhog sees its shadow, is there going to be six more weeks of winter?

Believe it or not, the answer to the overall question of whether animals can predict the weather is yes. Animals can feel and hear things that we humans cannot. Frogs can sense when rain is approaching, and they do indeed begin to croak more fervently; the croaking is the male frog's mating call. Most of them want to be parents, and with the rain coming there will be a lot of fresh water for the females to lay eggs.

Dogs, meanwhile, have a lot better sense of smell than we do, and can tell when rain is coming. If your dog suddenly appears to be tense or makes a run toward shelter, a storm has likely been sensed.

The groundhog telling how many weeks of winter are left, though, is just a folk story. Before accurate instruments were available to measure the weather, people would study animal behavior and would notice patterns. Sometimes the animal behavior was due to the impending weather; sometimes it was pure coincidence. For instance, farmers noticed that if it was going to rain, sheep would huddle together in a barn; this was more than coincidence. They also noticed that cows tended to lay down before a storm; this was only coincidence. The groundhog being able to tell how close spring is happens to be only coincidence.

The tradition of the groundhog being able to predict the weather came to the United States from German immigrants who settled in Pennsylvania. In fact. Punxsutawney Phil, the official groundhog, lives in Gobbler's Knob in Punxsutawney, Pennsylvania. (Phil and his wife Phyllis have a second house in the Punxsutawney Library and can be found there much of the year.) In Germany, the Germans had a hedgehog that made the prediction; when they got to the United States, they found the hedgehog's cousin, the groundhog, and gave him the duties. The legend says that Phil wakes up each year – his handlers wake him if he oversleeps – and sticks his head out of his burrow. If he sees his shadow, he goes back to bed for another six weeks because winter is far from over. If he does not see his shadow, then he goes about normal groundhog activities because spring is coming soon.

Phil began predicting weather in 1888 and has been wrong much, much more than he has been right. (To say that it is Phil who made these inadequate predictions is a bit of a stretch. Groundhogs live for six years maximum, so, needless to say, the original Punxsutawney Phil went to the Big Burrow in the Sky long ago. There have been several Phils through the years, even though people pretend it is the same one.) Legend, though, says that Phil has been given a special beverage by the Inner Circle – those mysterious men in top hats you see each year at the ceremony – that allow him to have another seven years of life each time he takes a sip.

The groundhog seeing its shadow predicts six more weeks of winter, but if you flip a coin you are just as likely to be right about winter hanging on. Although you can't trust the groundhog for being accurate, watching the groundhog on February 2 is a curious custom firmly rooted in American culture. Most Americans know they can't believe what the groundhog has to say, but they are still curious about what the groundhog has to say.

FUN FACTS

The Groundhog Day celebration has roots in the Roman Catholic Church service, Candlemas. On February 2, Christian priests in Europe in the Middle Ages would bless and pass out candles. If it was cloudy on Candlemas Day, spring was coming; if it was sunny on Candlemas Day, it would be winter for another six weeks.

Sharks can sense a hurricane coming, and they will dive deeper than normal in response.

Phil was just "the groundhog" until 1961, when he received his name. (He was likely named for Prince Philip, Duke of Edinburgh.)

Chapter 9
Why Do We Give Cards on Valentine's Day?

Have you ever passed notes in class?

You don't have to answer that aloud. I know that note-passing is against the rules, and you would never do anything against the rules. It's just that if you have never passed a note, you won't be able to relate to what I am going to say.

I confess that I have handed a note a couple of times up-and-down a row. I will also confess that I have received a note or two. One of my favorites was when my crush and her best friend from elementary school sent me a note in fifth grade that read, "We like you. Do you like us? Check 'yes' or 'no'." I, of course, checked 'yes' and passed it back.

St. Valentine was a Roman Catholic physician and priest who lived around 200 C.E. in the Roman Empire. When the Roman emperor, known today as Claudius the Cruel, declared that soldiers could not be married – he decreed this because he thought marriage made the soldiers less patriotic because they put family above country, St. Valentine would marry soldiers to their sweethearts in secret, right before the men shipped out. Of course, word got out, and he was arrested. Claudius the Cruel offered to spare him if he would simply submit to the Roman gods, but St. Valentine refused; in fact, he tried to convert the emperor to Christianity. One story claims that while he was in jail, St. Valentine healed the jailor's daughter of her blindness; the two became good friends -some would say the two of them fell in love. As St. Valentine was about to be executed, he slipped the jailor a note and asked that it be delivered to his girlfriend. The jailor took the note and delivered it. The note said, "Love always, your Valentine." St. Valentine was beheaded on February 14, 270.

The Roman Catholic Church made a feast day in his honor and chose to hold it each year on the day he was beheaded; it was a pragmatic choice because it gave Christians something to celebrate while the rest of the nation celebrated the traditional pagan festival Lupercalia which was focused more on lust than love. People believed that the emotions came from the heart – today we know they come from the brain, and so the heart became associated with St. Valentine. (It was also associated with him because of his being a physician.)
The original Valentine's heart was likely butt-shaped and green; it was the same shape as ours today but a different color. It was green to symbolize an undying love, just as evergreen trees are said to live forever, and was based on a green ivy leaf with that shape. Over the years, the heart turned to red, the color of passion.

Today, we still send Valentine's Day greetings to family and friends, often with cards with hearts on them. Even if you normally text, I suspect that you carry on the tradition of hand-signing a card. Today, those cards of affection we send are called "valentines" in honor of St. Valentine.

FUN FACTS

The winged god with a bow and arrow is Cupid, the son of the love goddess Venus.

Over one billion Valentine's cards are distributed on Valentine's Day worldwide.

The person receiving the most Valentine's Day cards in most communities is the schoolteacher.

Chapter 10
Why Do We Pinch People Not Wearing Green on St. Patrick's Day?

Have you ever seen someone about to go deer hunting? They put on camouflage so that they blend into the woods and the deer can't see them. The deer, though, cannot see the color orange either, so the hunter makes sure to wear orange so that other hunters don't shoot at him.

Let's put our conversation about camouflage and orange on hold for a minute and talk about the color green. Green is to be worn on St. Patrick's Day; it's not in an official document, but custom states that if you forget to wear green on March 17, you are likely going to get reminded throughout the day. People aren't just going to verbally tell you about it, they are also going to take a chunk of your skin and pinch it.

March 17 is St. Patrick's Day, the day we celebrate Ireland and everything Irish. For religious people, it is a time to remember St. Patrick, the man who is said to have rid Ireland of all its snakes. For families, it is a time to trace one's family heritage and share stories of days past. For many youths of all cultures, it is a time to learn about Irish folk tales, dance Irish jigs, and try traditional Irish grub such as corned beef and cabbage. For many adults, it is simply a day to have fun, drink green beverages, and hang out with friends. But does any of this justify pinching someone for not wearing green?

According to legend, leprechauns come out on St. Patrick's Day to celebrate. Normally leprechauns keep to themselves, but on this day they are active throughout human communities. They are tiny and fast, so it is unlikely you will see one. The question is, will they see you? Leprechauns have a color-blindness for green. Therefore, anyone wearing green is invisible to them, just as the person wearing camouflage is invisible to the deer. Believe me, you want to be invisible to leprechauns on this day. One of the ways the leprechauns entertain themselves is to sneak up on a person and pinch them. The only people they can't pinch are those people they can't see; the one's wearing green. Therefore, if you are not wearing green, you are going to be pinched by a leprechaun.

When a friend pinches you, the friend is reminding you that unless you put on green, you are going to get pinched repeatedly on St. Patrick's Day. The friend is right, but in my experience, the pinching will not be by leprechauns; it will be by other so-called friends warning you that you are leprechaun bait unless you put on some green.

FUN FACTS

St. Patrick himself was originally linked to blue.

St. Patrick's Day is a party day in the church season of Lent, normally a very somber time.

Ireland is nicknamed "the Emerald Isle" because of all its greenery.

Chapter 11
Why Was April 22 Chosen to be Earth Day?

Have you ever heard the slogan, "Every day is Earth Day"? It means that we are to celebrate the earth and strive to be a good steward of it not just one day of the year – appropriately named Earth Day – but every day of the year. This raises the question, why was April 22 chosen to be celebrated as Earth Day in the United States?

Unlike many holidays which have their roots in festivals of past generations, Earth Day was scheduled to be at an ideal time for its desired audience to participate. The desired audience were participants in the American education system ranging from elementary school to college. The founders believed that this young generation was the one that could make a difference in the future and then pass on earth stewardship to those that followed. Schools typically close for spring break at either the literal middle of the semester or at Easter, so the founders wanted to wait until after these dates. School, meanwhile, often ended in very early May for some schools, so it had to be before students were too engrossed in studying for finals to participate. Therefore, they settled upon the date of April 22.

Earth Day may have begun as an American holiday, but it quickly caught on world-wide. Unlike many holidays, Earth Day is not sponsored by the federal government of any nation. Different countries celebrate it on different days; not everyone follows the U.S.' lead and uses April 22.

There is no one right way to celebrate Earth Day. Each community must decide what it will do. Some people band together to clean out a stream, some plant a tree, some go on a hike to learn about nature, some tour a recycling plant, and some do solar experiments. The goal of Earth Day is to raise awareness about issues affecting the earth – climate change, air pollution, over-population, pesticide runoff, removing too many trees – and what can be done to resolve these issues. Although these issues should be discussed every day, in the hecticness of life, we often need a reminder to discuss these and to take action.

The younger generation did indeed accept that challenge to keep an Earth Day each year, and Earth Day has been celebrated for over 50 years now. Many challenges have been met – the air is much cleaner than in 1970 and the highways have far less litter, but other challenges remain – and so does the celebration of Earth Day.

FUN FACTS

The first Earth Day was in 1970; over 2 million people around the world celebrated it.

Gaylord Nelson, a senator from Wisconsin, is considered the founder of Earth Day.

The internationalizing of Earth Day was led by Denis Hayes; 192 countries celebrate Earth Day.

The U.S. Environmental Protection Agency was formed in response to Earth Day.

Chapter 12
Why Do We Carve Jack-O-Lanterns for Halloween?

Have you ever wondered why a Jack-O-Lantern is called a "Jack-O-Lantern" instead of a "Brad-O-Lantern" or "Kevin-O-Lantern"? Also, why do we even carve pumpkins in the first place?

Believe it or not, the first products to be carved into lanterns were not pumpkins, they were turnips and beets. The tradition of carving vegetables around Halloween began in Europe. When Europeans migrated to the United States, they brought it with them. In the United States, pumpkins were much more plentiful – plus bigger, and so they became the carving vegetable of choice. But why carve vegetables at all?

The carved vegetable was originally a lantern whose light was meant to scare away evil spirits that would come out in the dark. Just in case the evil spirits weren't intimidated by the light, many vegetables were given scary faces meant to intimidate the spirits. Evil spirits were thought to roam the countryside around late October, especially October 31. In the Celtic calendar, October 31 marked the end of autumn but, more importantly, the beginning of a new year. The Celtics pictured each year as if it were a scroll that had been sewn to the previous year; At the seams of the year, spirits could progress from the other world to earth. Some spirits took advantage of this and sought to haunt those who wronged them or to make amends to someone they had wronged. The spirit's time was limited, though, if one wanted to return to the other side, for the portal between realms was only open briefly. Those who feared being haunted by spirits tried to scare away all spirits with the lit carved vegetable, called a Jack-O-Lantern.

The Jack-o-lantern is named after a trickster named Stingy Jack. Jack was a mean, but smart man. One day Stingy Jack had been talking to the devil, telling the devil that the devil had no power. The devil, full of pride, assured Jack that he did have power. Jack taunted that he couldn't change himself into a coin. The devil changed himself into a coin to prove it. Jack immediately snatched the coin and tossed it in his pocket beside his silver cross; the devil was powerless. The devil bargained with Jack for his freedom, and they agreed that if Jack freed him then the devil could never put Jack in Hell. One day, Jack died, and God said he was too mean to go to Heaven and sent him to Hell. The devil, though, couldn't take him either. Therefore, the devil gave him a lantern, tossed him a coal, and told him he had to roam the earth forever. People called him Jack of the Lantern. "Jack of The Lantern" soon became "Jack-O-Lantern." At first the term meant the whole person and the lantern, but eventually it came to mean just the lantern itself.

FUN FACTS

The term "Jack O-Lantern" was used as early as 1663; it originally was applied to night watchmen who carried lanterns.

The United States grows over 1.5 billion pounds of pumpkins each year.

A carved pumpkin will last ten days if kept in temperatures ranging from 52-55 degrees Fahrenheit (11.1 – 12.7 degrees Celsius).

Chapter 13
Why Do the VFW (Veterans of Foreign Wars) Give Poppies on Veterans Day?

Last year on Veterans Day my mom and I came to a stoplight on a suburban street. The light turned red, so we stopped. Standing in front of the stop light were war veterans; some holding cans and others holding a bouquet of red poppies. One came up to the car and gave each of us a red plastic poppy with a green wire stem; he then shook a canister, and my mom gave him the change in the car change holder.

What a strange ritual, I thought! Believe it or not, though, this or something like this happens every year on November 11 not only in the United States, but in England, France, and other countries. It is a way to remember World War One, The Great War, as it was called then. When it ended in 1918, World War One had created the most death and destruction of any war in human history. In particular, it had ruined entire forests and taken many lives in France and Belgium. Despite the destruction, poppies had begun to appear in the field, signifying hope for the future.

To remember the Great War and to raise money to assist soldiers, veterans in the United States, United Kingdom, and France all distribute poppies to the public on Veterans Day. (In the United States, some also do it on Memorial Day, the last Monday of May.) Veterans Day, by the way, is always on November 11, the day that World War One ended.

Because poppies don't last year-round, artificial flowers are usually distributed instead of real ones. The flower's accomplishment of flourishing and adding beauty to a desolate landscape were the main reasons it was selected. When Canadian army officer John McCrae had seen the poppies in the field where the Second Battle of Ypres took place a few months after the battle, he was so moved that he wrote the poem "In Flanders Field" to celebrate the many soldiers who lay buried beneath them. His poem was published in *Punch* in 1915, and its fame spread so people on both sides of the Atlantic Ocean were aware of both the poem and poppies by 1918 when the war ended. To this day, poppies are still used to both remember the war and to inspire hope in dark times.

FUN FACTS

The first Veterans Day occurred exactly one year after World War I ended and was originally called Armistice Day.

In 1954, following the end of both World War II and the Korean War, the U.S. Congress changed Armistice Day, which honored only World War I veterans, to Veterans Day to honor all military veterans.

Veterans Day honors those who have served in the military; Memorial Day honors those who died.

Chapter 14

Why Do We Decorate Christmas Trees?

One of my favorite times of the year is the Christmas season. However, I must admit, that is also when people do some very weird things. For instance, can you imagine bringing a tree into your house and then decorating it at any other time of the year; people would think you were insane – but, at Christmas, that is perfectly normal behavior.

Well, within reason. Bringing an elm, sycamore, walnut, or apple tree would be abnormal. It has to be a fir tree, spruce tree, or pine tree, something that is green. This fact is our first clue that there must be a special meaning associated with the tree – and there is.

The evergreen tree represents eternal life. In reality, evergreen trees do die; it may take them 1,500 years, but they do die. However, to see them, you would not think so. Whereas other trees drop their leaves and appear to be dead in winter, the evergreen tree maintains its appearance year-round for year upon year.

Although Christians are quick to point out that the tree is a reminder that Jesus died on a cross made from a tree and that the green tree symbolizes eternal life – they even tie greens into a circle that has no beginning or end, the Christmas wreath, the concept of the green representing eternal life occurred long before Christianity. Pagans realized that the days got shorter and shorter until December 21, and then the days got longer. To celebrate the fact that the sun god had almost died but then recovered, the Egyptians held a winter feast in which they brought palm leaves into their home to signify the victory. Meanwhile, the Romans had a festival to Saturn, the Goddess of Agriculture, every December 21-25 to celebrate that she had decided to return another year.

Although the bringing of greenery into the home was common since early days, the concept of decorating the tree did not get underway until 1510 in Riga, Latvia. Someone shared the idea in 1531 in a brochure created by the newly invented printing press; the idea spread quickly after that. Queen Victoria made having a Christmas tree a tradition in the United Kingdom; Franklin Pierce, the fourteenth President of the United States, made it a White House tradition in the United States in 1856.

Candles were used to decorate trees in the 1600s. For the Christians, this reflected that Jesus was the light. In 1882, Thomas Edison's assistant, Edward Johnson, produced the concept of electric Christmas tree lights, and by 1890 these were being mass produced. To complement the Christ-theme, Christians often hung red balls, signifying the holy blood of Jesus. Today, numerous themes – from Star Wars to NASCAR – can be found on trees.

FUN FACTS

Approximately 35 million Christmas trees are sold annually in the United States; approximately 60,000 are sold around the world.

The first artificial tree was made in Germany in the 1800s. The trees were made of goose feathers that had been dyed green.

A Christmas tree needs to be six to ten years-old before harvesting.

Chapter 15
Why Do We Light Candles on a Birthday Cake?

Have you ever stopped to think how insane a visitor from another planet must think that we are? For instance, if someone turns thirteen, that person is likely to receive a cake as a gift. That cake, though, has thirteen candles on it. And the candles are lit! The recipient is expected to make a wish and then attempt to blow out all the candles. The recipient then puffs, blowing who knows what onto the cake. Everybody cheers, though, as smoke fills the air, and each participant eagerly waits for a share of the cake. In our society, this is deemed as normal behavior. In other countries, giving someone a cake that is on fire, having them blow it out, and then expecting to have a piece of what was given to them that is now covered with their germs would not make sense. Does it even make sense to you when you stop and think about it? Why do we light candles? Why do we make wishes? Why do we sing "Happy Birthday"? And why do we share cake?

The birthday celebration is filled with superstition from past days. The concept of the birthday cake has its roots in ancient Greece. In Greece, round cakes were often made in honor of the Greek goddess, Artemis, - they looked like a full moon and, when lit, became a glowing full moon. When a person makes a wish and blows out the candles, the smoke takes the wish to the goddess; if the person does not blow out all the candles, one's wish will not come true.

One's birthday marked a trip around the sun for the birthday person, and this beginning/ end seam made one especially susceptible to evil spirits that could enter through the seams. Therefore, people sang boisterously and tooted noisemakers with the intent of scaring off the evil spirits. One of the reasons for having lots of friends around was to protect oneself from the evil spirits.

The modern birthday party can trace its roots to the 1700s in Germany. German Count Nikolaus Ludwig Von Zinzendorf had an extravagant festival in honor of his birthday in 1746; the modern birthday party parallels his celebration. The party included games, food, singing, and gift-opening.

FUN FACTS

Chinese people celebrate the moon goddess Heng O with rice cakes.

Traditionally, one candle is placed on the cake for each year that a person is alive.

The most popular day to have a birthday in the United States is October 5.

People are most likely to be born on Tuesday; least likely on Sunday

Chapter 16

Why Do People Throw Rice at the Bride and Groom at Weddings?

When I was a little boy, I remember my mom coming up to me at a wedding reception and telling me, "Come on." I had just finished my cake and punch. I set the cup and napkin down, she grabbed me by the hand, and then she led me outside to the front steps of the church. Other people were already there, all staring intently for the bride and groom.

My mom whisked me down the stairs and put some rice in my hands. "Throw this at the bride and groom," she whispered. I thought it was a weird request, but I noticed that everyone else outside also had handfuls of rice, so I figured she was being serious. I started to ask her why, but she just said, "Sh!" as mothers are sometimes prone to do.

For the next ten minutes, I laid in wait like an 1870s Western outlaw waiting for the train to round the bend. Finally, the bride and groom opened the church door and started through the line of well-wishers on both sides of them. As the rice started to fall down on them – everybody tossed it up gently and let it fall rather than hurling it like a 90-mile-per-hour baseball, the couple waved at their friends and family, smiling.

They got into a car which had the banner "Just married" on it, as well as a few cans tied to it. Well, I say they got in the car; that isn't exactly what happened. Somebody had stuffed it full of inflated balloons. Once the groom had removed several balloons and popped some others, they climbed into the car, waved joyfully, and drove off.

The tradition of throwing rice is in many religions, and those people who don't do it for religious reasons do it simply because it is a fun tradition. Whether Hindu or Christian, the rice is a thank you to God for life, food, and love. The thanks goes up; the blessings come down. For both the secular and the religious, the falling rice is intended to wish many children upon the couple.

Although the rice can be thrown as the couple leaves the church sanctuary after the ceremony, it is generally thrown as the couple leaves the church building itself. The noise from throwing the rice and the noise of the cans on the car are all meant to scare away evil spirits and to keep the couple safe. Whether you believe in evil spirits or not, it never hurts to make a little noise and to show you wish the bride and groom a happy future.

FUN FACTS

Raw rice is safe for birds; rice does NOT blow up in birds' stomachs.

Seeds, herbs, flowers, rose petals, bubbles, confetti, and just about anything else could be tossed or blown at the bride and groom should someone have a rice allergy.

Ancient Romans tossed wheat, not rice, at the bride and groom.

Chapter 17
Why Do Matadors Wave Red Flags?

Have you ever seen a professional bullfighter, or a rodeo clown try to get a bull's attention? To do so, they wave a red flag. Upon seeing the flag, the bull gets mad, usually digs its foot into the dirt, and then, after a couple of snorts, takes off to attack the flag. Have you ever wondered why bulls hate red flags so much?

Unbelievably, it is not the color red that the bulls despise. Bulls are colorblind to red; that is, one shade of red may appear to be a darker grey than another shade, but bulls cannot see the color. The cloth could be blue, yellow, or green, and it would get the same reaction from the bull.

What the bull senses is the sudden movement of the flag. Bulls are short-sighted; that is, they cannot make things out that are far from them. In this case, the bull can't tell if it is a flag or something else; he can just see movement. The movement makes the bull think that it is in danger, and, in a classic fight-or-flight response, a bull will charge the moving object. (If you ever find yourself in a field with a bull, simply move very, very slowly away from it; if you try to run, the bull is likely to charge at you.)

The red color of the flag is for the people who are watching. We humans can see red, and we have been taught to associate red with danger. Although the color red may not excite the bull, it does excite the audience. The red also stands out, making the movement of the cloth easy to find and easy to follow.

FUN FACTS

All creatures with hooves, not just bulls, are color-blind to red.

A bullfighter's red cape is called a capote or muleta.

Bullfighting in which a matador waved a red flag in front of a bull became a Spanish sport in the 1700s; it continues today, although many people perceive it as cruel to animals.

PART 3
CONTEMPORARY DAILY LIFE

Chapter 18

Why Do We Say "Hello" When Answering the Telephone?

Hello~

If I were to call you on the telephone, what would be the first thing you would say? Most people say, "Hello." Have you ever wondered why?

Believe it or not, this was not the greeting that Alexander Graham Bell, the inventor of the telephone, was encouraging people to say. Alexander Graham Bell believed that the proper greeting for answering the phone should be "Ahoy." "Ahoy" was a greeting sailors used, such as in the phrase, "Ahoy, matey."

The companies that provided telephone services wrote manuals to accompany the phones. Different companies had different recommendations. These ranged from "Are you ready to talk?," "Are you there?" and "What is wanted?" (Today, the latter would be considered downright rude.)

Thomas Edison believed that "Hello" should be the way to greet someone when answering the phone. "Hello" was not an English word at that time; it had been a sound that hunters made when assembling their hunting party, including their dogs. He may or may not have been the person to come up with the idea, but he had the prestige to get it accepted.

Not only did phone companies produce manuals of how to use the telephone, but etiquette books were also published as well. "Hello" was considered formal and was to be used when greeting people on the street or on the phone. "Hi" was considered informal and could be used when greeting relatives and friends.

Society also had to agree on how to close a conversation. Guidebooks suggested signing off with "that is all" and "God bless" as well as "goodbye," the way most people close phone calls today.

FUN FACTS

Switchboard operators were originally known as Hello Girls.

"Hello" first appeared in the dictionary in 1883.

Thomas Edison was asked to make a telephone that would make the sound "hello" instead of a bell sound when someone called; he never did.

Chapter 19

Why Do We Shake Hands When Meeting People?

    Have you ever watched two dogs greet each other? They typically sniff each other's butts. I bet you would think I was strange if I came up to you and started to sniff your butt! However, we as humans have our own manner of greeting people – and it may not be all that much different.

    When I am introduced to somebody, I put out my right hand, take their outstretched hand into my hand firmly, and then shake my arm two or three times before releasing their hand. This is a ritual we know as "shaking hands," and it is used in a wide variety of settings in many cultures throughout the world. Have you ever wondered why we shake hands?

The custom likely dates back over four thousand years to the days when clan chiefs – call them kings if you want – and mighty warriors would go to meet the clan chief of another tribe for a high stakes meeting. The two men – it was almost always men – would walk out to each other. They would hold their right hand out – it was their right hand because that was their dominant hand - so that the other person could see that they did not have a weapon. When they met face to face, they then put their hands together and shook; this was to jiggle loose any weapon that might be hidden in the other's sleeve. (These guys didn't trust each other – and for good reason.)

Shaking hands became a tradition for men. In terms of men and women, men used to kiss the woman's hand, but today women are generally treated equally with men. If a woman is uncomfortable shaking hands, she will not put her hand out, but will instead nod and verbally greet the other person.

Other etiquette has also evolved over shaking hands. For instance, you should not hand a person a "dead fish," but you also should not try to squeeze their hand so tight you might break one of their bones. A lack of etiquette indicates that one is either uncouth or believes one is above the social ritual; either way, you will make a bad impression.

Earlier I made the comment that people are more similar to dogs than they realize. Did you know that most people will smell their hand that they shook hands with? They want to get a whiff of the other person. Just like other mammals, humans can learn about each other through scents. (I have never caught myself doing it, but social scientists believe most people do this and don't even realize they have done it.)

FUN FACTS

Around 1800 B.C.E. the king of Babylon began each year publicly shaking hands with a statue of a god.

Researchers have found that people are more likely to smell their shaking hand after shaking hands with someone of their own gender than with someone of the opposite sex.

Your body produces chemicals during a handshake that get on the other person; the chemicals – squalene and hexadecenoic acid – are the same chemicals cats and dogs use to attract each other.

Chapter 20

Why Do Soldiers Salute?

When one soldier sees another soldier, the lower ranking soldier is supposed to salute. This saluting is supposed to be a sign of respect.

It isn't always, though. I have watched some of my classmates stand in the hall, watch a teacher walk by, and then give a salute. The salute was given in jest, and it suggested anything but respect.

"To show respect" is a good answer, but not a great one. Afterall, respect can be shown in a lot of ways. Some people bow down before others (such as those respecting the King), and some kiss the other person's ring (such as those respecting the Pope). How did raising one's hand and putting it against one's face come to mean respect?

Different theories exist as to why this came about, and I believe all three have led to the gesture we have today. My favorite is that most people are right-handed, and, if they are going to harm anyone, they will hold a knife in their right hand. By opening their hand and clearly showing that nothing is in it, they are showing that they come in peace and have respect for the other person. The gesture of saluting has its roots back with ancient people.

A second theory says that knights in the Middle Ages gave us the custom. Knights wore body armor and, when they met a superior, they would raise their metal visor to say hello. When the age of metal visors ended, people retained the tradition of raising one's hand as if to raise a visor.

A third theory says that soldiers used to remove their hats to show respect, just as men today often remove their hat when a woman that they respect walks into the room. The soldiers' headgear was bulky, and it took time to take off and put on, so, instead of literally removing the headgear, the soldier simply moved their hand up to touch their cap to suggest that they would be willing to remove their headgear out of respect.

Regardless of which – if not all – theory is correct, saluting is ingrained into world-wide society. However, that does not mean that everybody salutes in the same way. If you look closely, you will see that the soldiers of some countries and sometimes even soldiers with different branches of military service within the same country, salute differently. For instance, the British Army and Air Force prefer their soldiers to salute so that the hand is pointing to the sky, but the British Navy prefers that their soldiers salute with the hand tilted down. (Sailors had dirty hands, and it was considered disrespectful to show one's dirty palm.) If you ever join the military, find out how you are to tilt your hand when saluting.

FUN FACTS

Civilians are not supposed to salute military personnel nor the flag.

If a child salutes a soldier as he walks past, the soldier will likely wave in reply.

Both veterans and plain-clothed service are allowed to salute the flag along with those currently serving in the U.S. military; everyone else should stand with their right hand over their heart to show respect.

Chapter 21

Why Do People Wear Monograms on Their Clothing?

When you get something nice and new, what do you do? If you are like me, you put your initials on it in a couple of places. (I usually place mine big so that they can be clearly seen so no one is tempted to innocently take my new gadget thinking it is theirs, and I also place them small and inconspicuous, so that if someone does take it and claim it is theirs, I can tell the teacher/authority where my initials are to prove that it's mine.)

Have you ever seen a piece of clothing, usually a shirt or a handkerchief, with two or more initials on it? Typically, these are the initials of the owner of the clothing item, although they can be the initials of the designer. Although there is no set way to monogram, in many cases, one letter is huge and the other two are smaller; the huge is the person's last name, the small letter on top and to the left is the person's first initial, and the second letter on top to the right is the person's middle initial; if the three letters are in a row, the first initial will be first, the last initial will be next and the biggest, and the middle initial will be third and the same size as the first initial.

Why do people get things monogrammed? One, it personalizes a gift. For instance, a piece of jewelry may look like any other piece of jewelry, but by monogramming it, it becomes unique – it can be clearly identified as belonging to the owner. Two, it promotes pride. Each of us is a brand, and, when people see our monogram, they know that it belongs to us. Three, it discourages thieves. No one wants to steal something with someone else's initials all over it.

Monograms likely began as a way to show ownership. Kings developed a monogram and would use that as their official seal; if the monogram were missing for an item, the product was a fake. Coins had monograms on them to show they were authentic. Artists put their monograms on their works to reduce claims by forgers. Kings and queens often had their possessions – everything from swords to underwear – mixed with common people, and they wanted to ensure they got theirs back.

My brother used to work at a summer residential camp. Each week, he and the other male camp staff would take their clothes to the camp laundress to wash. Because she would wash all of their jeans together, it was important that they each marked their clothing with permanent markers. After she had washed them, she would then sort them into piles for each person to pick up. Monograms are both practical and decorative.

FUN FACTS

At weddings, the wedding cake may have the first initial of the groom, the family initial, and the first initial of the bride.

Monograms often become business logos. (Think of Rolls Royce, for example.)

A human can make approximately 2,000 stitches per square inch; a machine can make 7,500 stitches per square inch – both give embroidered monograms great detail.

Chapter 22

Why Do People Speak Different Languages?

"Hello."
"Hallo."
"Salam."
"Guten Tag."
"Yasou."
"Hola."

I just said, "Hello" in six different languages – English, Dutch, Persian, German, Greek, and Spanish. How many were you able to figure out?

Wouldn't it be nice if everyone spoke the same language? Apparently at one time in the past, people did. Whether you believe people came from apes or descended from Adam, both evolution and Christianity speculate there was a very small group of humans at first, and that gradually this small group multiplied and spread across the land.

So why aren't we speaking the same language today? The people who study language – "linguists," offer several reasons. First, there is the fact that different people need different words because of new things they encounter. For instance, the Eskimo needed words for snow while the Sahara nomad needed words for sand. Human society has root languages that have flowered into other languages and dialects. For instance, the Romans may have spoken Latin, but Latin has diverged into Spanish, France, and Italian. Meanwhile, English began as a Germanic language, and now we have numerous dialects – The people in England do not speak as the people in the United States, and even the people in Massachusetts do not speak the way of someone from Alabama.

Two, language became a way to unite a tribe. Just as we are united by school mascots and shared histories, tribes were united by the language and symbols they used. Anyone who did not know the language was an outsider. Even in clubs today, the insiders know the secret password that outsiders do not know.

People of different languages came into contact with each other through trade and war, and therefore the words of one language found its way into another language. That is also why people sometimes have two terms for the same item.

Languages also got corrupted by dialects. Today, many people drop their "g"s in words such as "lying," and most of us don't put the "b" in "climb" like our ancestors did. The English we speak today is different from the English spoken in the times of King James and Shakespeare and is very, very different from what was spoken in 1100 A.D. when *Beowulf* was written.

FUN FACTS

Approximately 4,000 new words are added to the dictionary yearly.

Unlike many countries, the United States does not have an official language.

"You" and "I" are the most common English words.

Chapter 23

Why Do People Wear Their Wedding Bands on Their Left Third Finger?

Have you ever noticed at traditional wedding ceremonies how the wedding ring is always placed on the third finger, the ring finger, the one next to the pinky? Have you ever wondered why that finger is chosen and not any of the others? If you said it is placed there because of tradition, you would be correct. However, the tradition had to start somewhere and there must be a reason for it.

The tradition of wedding rings dates back to ancient Greece and ancient Egypt. The ring is a circle, and it symbolizes eternal love. The concept of wearing the ring on the third finger came about because ancient health care workers believed that the center for love was located in the heart and because they believed a vein, the vena amoris, ran from the heart directly to that finger. (Modern medicine has concluded emotions such as love reside in the brain and not the heart; they have also concluded there is no vena amoris.) The tradition, though, was firmly entrenched in European culture by that time, however.

Most people – it was only women who wore wedding rings in ancient cultures, but today both men and women wear them - wear their wedding band on their left hand, the hand that is closest to the heart. In certain cultures – Eastern Europe, Scandinavia, India, Central America, and South America, people tend to wear them on the right ring finger; the right hand is usually the dominant hand, and therefore people in favor of this position claim that it is more readily seen.

In the United States, engagement rings are also worn on the third finger. If one chooses to keep wearing the engagement ring after marriage, the engagement ring is usually placed on top of the wedding band; hence the wedding band is closest to the heart. Meanwhile, in some other countries, the engagement ring is worn on the right ring finger, and, after the marriage, moved to the left hand to be on top of the wedding band.

The wedding ring is a symbol of one's love for someone else and politely tells would-be suitors that one is taken. The ring is a token, an item that communicates nonverbally. However, don't rush to judgments. Some married people do not wear their wedding ring on their ring finger – it may interfere with their work, so they wear it on a necklace; they may be allergic to the metals in it; they may not be comfortable; or they simply don't want to follow tradition. Likewise, some people put a ring on that finger even if they are not married; for instance, single women in a cocktail lounge who do not want men to come up to flirt with them will put a ring on the ring finger to convey the "buzz off" message – and some two-timing men will slide their wedding ring off their finger and into their pocket to let the patrons know that they are available.

Rings are just one of many things that tell people about us. That cross on a necklace says that one is a Christian (or just likes the cross shape), the baseball cap with the Kansas City Chiefs logo implies that one likes the Kansas City Chiefs American football team, and the shirt with the polo logo suggests that you have middle-to-upper class tastes. It's ironic, but, like it or not, our clothes and accessories tend to reveal a lot about us.

FUN FACTS

Wedding rings were traditionally made of pure gold; white gold is the most common metal used today.

The groom presented the lady with a ring not just to show his love, but to show that he was capable of financially providing for her.

The custom of men wearing wedding rings began in World War II; the ring was a way for the married soldier to remember his wife back home.

Chapter 24

Why Do U.S. Citizens Have a Social Security Number, and What Does My Social Security Number Say About Me?

If you take Social Security Number 585-29-6789 and subtract Social Security Number 483-22-2567, do you get Social Security Number 102-07-4222?

Of course not. Social Security numbers aren't real numbers of value; they are names. Just like the quarterback on an American football team may be 12 and a defensive lineman is 82. Instead of knowing us by our name, computers know us as a number.

The original purpose of the Social Security Number (SSN) was to be able to track a person's income and the number of years that a person worked. The income one earns and the amount one pays into social security, influences how much disability benefits one can collect, when one can retire, and how much Social Security will pay upon retirement.

Today, the SSN is used for much more than just work associated with Social Security. The number has become a personal identifier, and you will need it to prove you are a citizen, to set up a checking account at the bank, pay taxes, to get a student loan, and numerous other activities.

You will have the same SSN all your life unless someone steals your identity. When you get a job, you will want to make sure that your employer has the correct social security number on file – mine did not; there was a typographical error. Your SSN is unique to you; no one else has it.

Your SSN is really three numbers – an area number, a group number, and a serial number. In 1936 when the SSN came into being, the first three digits were tied to particular regions of the country, just as zip codes are today; today, those first three numbers mean nothing, they are totally random. The group numbers, meanwhile, used to refer to specific filing cabinets; in the days before computers, everything was filed in a filing cabinet. The last four digits were always randomly assigned.

If you see an SSN that was assigned before 2011 when pure randomization started, you can probably figure out where they lived at the time they applied for an SSN. Otherwise, you can't learn much about a person based on their SSN.

FUN FACTS

Over 5.5 million new SSNs are given each year.

Since 1936, 420,000,000 SSNs have been assigned.

John David Sweeney received the first SSN in history in 1936; it was 055-09-0001

CHAPTER 25

Why Does Lady Justice Wear a Blindfold?

Have you ever been blindfolded? I used to play Blind Man's Bluff and smash-the-pinata, and both required blindfolds. If you have not been blindfolded, I suggest you try it. Have a friend tie a cloth over your eyes so that you cannot see through it, over it, or under it – no peeking. Next, have your friend take you by the hand, spin you around, and then walk you around the yard. It likely won't take you long to lose your bearings. Finally, stand still and listen to the world around you. You'll find that our sense of hearing is likely sharper and that you can't tell details such as a speaker's skin color.

Lady Justice wears a blindfold for that exact reason – she does not want to know a person's skin color, income status, or status in society – she wants to listen carefully to the details of the case. Lady Justice wears a blindfold so that she is not biased by the trappings of society that she could see.

Lady Justice's blindfold is relatively new. She began wearing it around 1500 when the Renaissance began. Lady Justice herself, though, goes back to ancient Egypt and ancient Greece. In those societies, her impartiality was shown in the fact that she was a maiden; people in the Renaissance, though, were not as acquainted with that symbol, so to reinforce the symbolism of impartiality, the blindfold was added.

Although Lady Justice is a world-wide symbol, she is often in attire that reflects the local culture. For instance, in the United States, she is often dressed similarly to the Statue of Liberty. Although her dress varies from country to country, she always carries an exposed double-edged sword and scales with her.

The double-edge-ness of the sword is a reminder that she is intent on ruling for the right party, regardless of which side of the courtroom that happens to be. The sword is unsheathed, showing that she is a person of action; it also reflects that she has nothing to hide. The sword is used to protect the innocent person and is used as a threat to make the guilty follow-through with restitution. It is also a reminder that justice can be swift and final.

In the hand that is not carrying the sword, Lady Justice carries a set of scales. (Typically, the scales are in the left hand and the sword is in her right hand, but sometimes the scales and the sword are reversed.) The scales are what she uses to weigh the two sets of evidence in the case. The scales are perfectly balanced, reflecting that she has no bias prior to hearing the evidence. Each side presents evidence that it is in the right; she then weighs the pros and the cons in her scales and determines which has more merit.

Lady Justice represents the morality of the justice system. You can see statues of Lady Justice outside most courtrooms, not only in the United States, but around the world. She serves as a reminder of how justice should be dispensed.

FUN FACTS

The first time Lady Justice was seen with a blindfold in a work of art was in Hans Gieng's Fountain of Justice in Berne, Switzerland, in 1543.

The Romans had a temple dedicated to the forerunner of Lady Justice, Justitia; although Justitia was pictured as a goddess, most Romans viewed her as a concept rather than an actual being.

Lady Justice is often pictured with her sister Prudentia (Prudence) who holds a mirror and a snake; Prudentia urges self-discipline and self-control.

PART 4
FOOD
AND
HEALTH

Chapter 26

Why Do Doughnuts Have a Hole in the Middle?

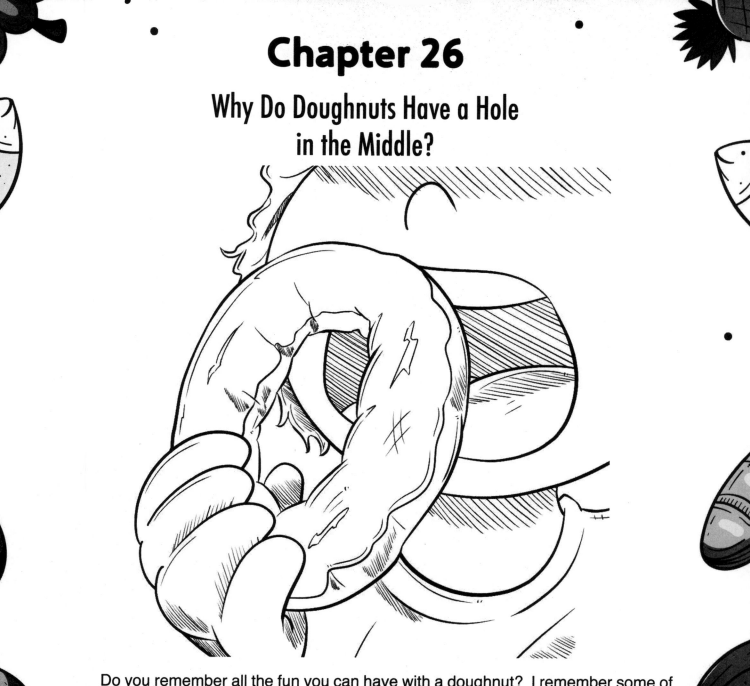

Do you remember all the fun you can have with a doughnut? I remember some of the fun I've had. I don't encourage you to do this because you might get in trouble, but I used to take two doughnuts and wear them like a pair of glasses, showing off at the table until I had everybody's attention or until my mom would say, "Quit playing with your food." Doughnuts – thanks to the holes inside them – provided hours of entertainment. But why are there holes in doughnuts?

To be fair to doughnut makers, I should make it clear that so-called experts claim that not all doughnuts have holes. They point to the jelly-filled pastries and the cream-filled pastries, and they observe that these are hole-less. While I agree that these are hole-less, I question their definition; just because something is sold at a doughnut shop does not make it a doughnut any more than a lightbulb sold at a grocery store makes it a food item. Where I grew up, cream-filled pastries were Long Johns, and the jelly-filled ones were Jelly Pastries; to qualify as a doughnut it has to have a hole in it.

Many – if not all, depending on whose definition you use, doughnuts do have holes. These holes are intentionally there. You might be inclined to think the missing part is missing because doughnut makers wanted to use the dough for something else, but there is a better reason – the doughnuts have a hole so that they cook better. Doughnuts without jelly, cream or another filling have dough in the middle; they are especially thick and doughy, in order for them to cook thoroughly, air must be able to reach the center; the hole allows the air to do exactly that. If you don't want filling but also don't want a hole in your doughnut, you can make an extremely thin pancake light doughnut that will cook all the way through.

The term doughnut likely came about because of Hanson Gregory, an eighteenth-century sailor, and he was likely inspired by his mom. She made him a dough cake with nuts in it to take on the journey. When other sailors asked what he was eating, he said, "Dough and nuts;" this was quickly shortened to "doughnuts."

FUN FACTS

Native Americans were eating fried pastries similar to doughnuts before doughnuts were even thought about.

The doughnut can trace its roots to Dutch colonists in New York City who made a pancake-like pastry - "olykoeks" which translates into English as "oily cakes;" as the cakes got bigger over time, holes had to be added so it would cook thoroughly.

"Doughnut holes" may or may not be made from the dough taken from the center of a doughnut; circles of fresh dough may have been fried instead.

Chapter 27

Why Do Fortune Cookies Always get My Fortune Right?
How Could They Know?

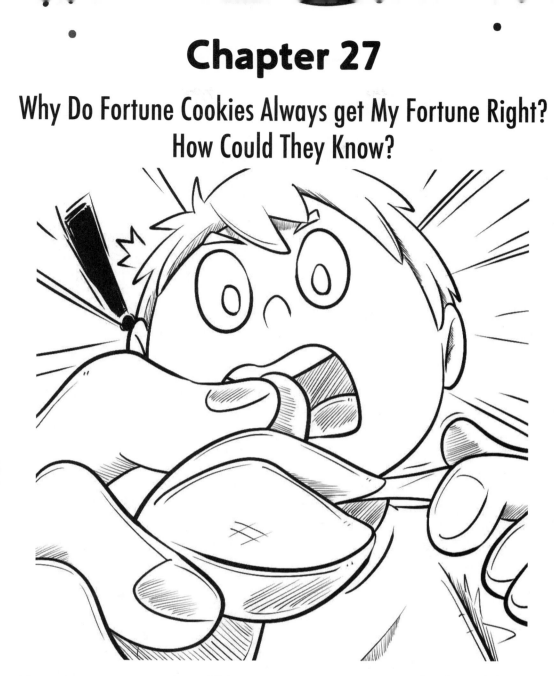

Have you ever gone to a Chinese restaurant, ate your food, and then have the waiter bring a fortune cookie for each person when presenting the bill? If you have, you likely broke the cookie in half, unfolded the fortune, read the fortune, and then ate the cookie. I know some people leave the fortune on the table, but I always take mine with me and, at the end of the day, I ponder if it came true – and in all cases it either came true that day or within the next couple of days. It was uncanny!

I don't believe in superstition; I also don't believe they were spying on me prior to my going to the restaurant. Different fortune cookies have different fortunes inside – one company that prints fortunes for the cookies has a data bank of over 15,000 fortunes upon which to draw, so how did the waiter know which cookie to give me? I had a mystery on my hands.

A fortune cookie begins its life just as any other cookie; it is round dough that is placed in the oven to cook. When it is cooked, the fortune is placed in its center, and then it is folded. Once the dough hardens, the cookie will keep its shape.

Although you may not realize it when you read it, the fortunes are very vague. For instance, "You will meet a stranger" is very vague; it doesn't tell when or where. Hence, when someone you don't know speaks to you, you have confirmation that the fortune is correct.

Psychologists call this confirmation bias; they claim that people try to interpret the event so that it matches what the fortune tag said would happen. They are essentially saying that because we expect to see something, we do see it.

The confirmation bias goes beyond fortune cookies. The theory states that if you think the world is a bad place, you will find reasons to justify your belief. However, if you are a positive thinker, you will find reasons to justify that belief. Everybody, so the theory goes, is looking through sunglasses; we see reality, but it is a tinted reality.

I'll admit that maybe I have confirmation bias – I expected to find that the fortunes predicted by fortune cookies were not magical, and that is indeed what I found. I'll let you decide for yourself. In the meantime, I am going to enjoy eating some more; just because I don't believe what the fortune in them says doesn't mean that I don't enjoy reading it or that I dislike the cookies' taste!

FUN FACTS

Over three billion fortune cookies are made each year.

The fortune cookie was invented in California around 1890, not China, by Asian immigrants.

Fortune cookies get their unique tastes from vanilla and sesame oil.

Chapter 28

Why Do We Eat Dessert Last Instead of First?

Do your parents let you stay up later than your younger sibling? If they do, my guess is that they let you do things that you can't do when your younger sibling is awake. In my household, I got to stay up a half-hour later than my younger sister, and in that half hour my parents and I would often play Clue, a game that I enjoyed that was too advanced for my sister.

The reason dessert is served last is very similar logic. In the days of Elizabethan England, sugar had been discovered in the New World. Sugar, though, was very, very expensive, and it was something that only the rich people could afford – ironically, it was the rich people who also got black teeth, rotting teeth, and cavities. In many cases the household staff would dine with the lord and lady of the house. After the meal, the lord and lady would retire to another room, where they enjoyed dessert in private. Eating dessert after a meal became a tradition.

Eating dessert last is a biological necessity for some people; they get sick if they eat dessert items on an empty stomach. Even for these people, though, dessert itself is not a biological necessity.

If dessert were a biological necessity, every culture would have dessert items; unbelievably, some cultures do not have a dessert course. However, dessert has become so commonplace in most cultures that most people look forward to it. I have heard many people say that "I'm full, but I'll make room for dessert," and there is truth in that statement. Whereas the taste buds may have tired of the main course, they get enthused when a new taste begins.

Many families keep the tradition of dessert after a meal because it encourages young children to eat healthy. My mom has told me many times, "If you don't clean your plate, you can't have any cookies." Dessert is one's reward.

Dessert has a bad reputation. Researchers have found that those people who eat dessert are much more likely to want sweets as adults and are therefore more prone to be overweight. Dessert in moderation, though, can be a good thing. A dark chocolate cake, for example, can help lower one's blood pressure and decrease the odds of having a stroke. Dessert has emotional benefits too; many people receive great pleasure from eating dessert. For them, dessert brings happiness, and it makes life more enjoyable.

Does dessert have to be eaten last? No. However, if you want to save the best for last, you'll likely want to keep dessert at the end of the meal.

FUN FACTS

"Dessert" is French for "clear the table."

Although criticized for their use of sugar, desserts are a fun way to eat fruit.

In England, the dessert course is often called "pudding" instead of "dessert."

Chapter 29

Why Do We Have Two Eyes, But We Only See One Image?

If you would please, grab a couple of pens or pencils, remove the caps so that the points are exposed, and place one in your left hand and one in your right. With your left eye closed, try to bring the two pen tips to touch. Now try doing it with your right eye closed. Pretend each pen is a rocket and you want them to dock; you only get one try. Now try getting the tips of the two pens to touch with both eyes open. If you are like most people, you will do best on the third try when both eyes are open.

Our two eyes allow us to see depth. When you are using only one eye, the depth is lacking. The brain sees the vision from both eyes and places it into one picture. This depth is an evolutionary trait that makes humans great marksmen. It is something that we share with lions, tigers, leopards, and other predators, for it enables us to judge prey accurately.

Let's try another experiment. Close your right eye and carefully think about what you see. Next, close your left eye and carefully think about what you can see. Now look with both eyes.

If you looked carefully, you noticed certain things out of your left eye that you didn't see out of your right eye, and, likewise, you saw certain things from your right eye that you could not see from the left. When you have both eyes open, though, you can see it all. Although the two eyes overlap, they each see things that the other cannot.

In both of the exercises I had you do; your eye's retina took a picture of the image that it saw and then sent it to the brain through the optic nerve. The brain then put the two pieces together in a 3D image and added the details each eye had left out. Your brain then announced that this is what you are seeing.

FUN FACTS

Spiders have eight eyes; jellyfish have 24.

A chicken's eyes function independently of each other, just like our right and left hand do.

On the average adult, the space between the two retinas is approximately 7.6 centimeters.

Chapter 30

Why Do People Yawn . . .
And Why Is a Yawn So Contagious?

Have you ever been in a room, and someone yawned? Chances are, several other people in the room followed suit. Even the family dog might have yawned. You may not have consciously wanted to yawn, but you likely yawned too. Have you ever wondered why this happens?

A yawn is an involuntary gasping for air. When we yawn, we open our mouth, take in a big gulp of air, and then release it. Notice that it is involuntary; that is, we cannot stop it. The most we can do is cover our mouth with our hands and hope that nobody notices.

Different people offer different explanations for why people yawn, and based on my personal experience, I think that ALL are correct. Some psychologists say that we yawn when our brain is shifting gears from high energy to low energy; that is why you will yawn when you get bored or when you get ready for bed. If you don't get enough sleep, you are likely to be yawning the next day because your body is going to be trying to shut down to get some sleep. Other people say that we yawn to adjust our equilibrium; when I go up or down a mountain or ride in an airplane, I yawn to pop my ears. The yawning stretches my face, allowing my eardrums to stretch and adjust. Some researchers note that yawning stretches the face, and this allows blood to rush to the brain. Others believe that the inhaling of a gulp of oxygen helps to cool the brain. Still others have suggested that yawning is a form of communication, a prehistoric way to signify empathy.

This latter is the reason that we tend to yawn when we see someone else yawn. We are trying to show them that we acknowledge them and that they are accepted by us. According to this theory, yawning goes back further than language, and it has been hardwired into us through evolution. Yawning in response when somebody else yawns is nothing to be ashamed of; it shows that you are a caring human being.

FUN FACTS

The average yawn lasts for six seconds.

Human babies yawn in the womb.

Yawns are contagious at any time of the day.

Chapter 31

Why Does Kissing a Boo-Boo Make It Better?

Did you pay close attention to how this question is worded? If you notice, there is no question of doubt about whether it works; it is a question of wanting to know why it works.

Most of us have experienced having a boo-boo kissed and can testify that it does feel better after the kiss. Also, we have seen numerous kids crying for the whole neighborhood to hear lying in the street where they fell off their bike; once their mom comes and gives the boo-boo a kiss, the crying suddenly stops. We have seen kissing a boo-boo work many, many times!

Scientists, though, aren't sure that it works. They admit that saliva can kill a lot of germs, and that when the boo-boo is kissed the saliva is placed onto the raw skin. (To put it more scientifically, the nitrous oxide and the protein histatin in the saliva not only rinses the wound but kills a lot of deadly bacteria.) Human beings are mammals, and, just like other mammals, we are hard-wired to "lick our wounds" – literally as well as mentally.

Scientists, though, do not encourage this. Although the saliva has a lot of good bacteria and can kill germs, it also has bad bacteria that can infect the wound. Also, if the kisser is literally putting lips on the wound, the kisser is going to ingest a lot of the dirt and bacteria from the wound.

Most scientists believe that any positive effect seen from kissing a boo-boo is due to the fact that the child feels cared about at the time. According to them, the mother could stand on her head if that were interpreted as a form of caring; it is the fact that a psychological need, rather than a physical need, is met that stops people from crying once a boo-boo is kissed. A second, similar explanation, is that the act of kissing takes the child's mind off the wound, and therefore it is perceived as not hurting.

Scientists believe that the same psychological effect can be achieved with a much more sanitary approach than kissing a wound. They advise using soap and water to clean a wound and then, if needed, adding an antiseptic cream. (Who knows; if animals had access to soap, water, and antiseptic, perhaps they too wouldn't lick a wound either.) If this act of caring is done by a parent or someone the wounded person respects, scientists believe the psychological outcome will be achieved.

FUN FACTS

Never let a pet lick your wound.

The muscle responsible for the lips puckering to give a kiss is called the orbicularis oris.

When mom kisses a wound, between 10 million and 1 billion bacteria are released; some of these are germ fighting bacteria and others are germy bacteria.

Chapter 32

Why Do Pills Often Have a Cotton Ball on Top of Them?

Have you ever taken the lid off a bottle of pills, broken the foil seal on the bottle, and then discovered, instead of looking at pills, you were looking at a huge wad of cotton? If you are like me, that got you wondering, why is that cotton wad in that pill bottle?

The most obvious reason for it being there is to cushion the pills during shipping. If it were not for the cotton, some pills might break, and people might put the wrong pieces of pill together, resulting in a dosage that could make them sick. The cotton, then, helps keep pills from breaking and helps save lives.

If the cotton is there because the bottle is too big, why don't the manufacturers make the bottle the correct size? Not only would this save cotton, but it would also save plastic. Believe it or not, the reason the bottle is too big for the pills is again safety related – the label needs to be printed large enough that people can read the important details on it.

Manufacturers also have a more-self-serving reason for making their bottles big – the bottles will grab people's attention and generate sales. Grocery stores often have eye-catching bottles right at the checkout line, encouraging spontaneous purchase, which is a win for both the grocery store and the manufacturer. Also, there is only so much room on a grocery store shelf, and a larger bottle size means less room for competition.

Unbelievably, an environmental reason for the larger size bottle with mostly air and cotton in it can be given too. Although environmentalists might cringe at the extra plastic required to make the bottle, the larger bottles are much more likely to be recycled by consumers than the little ones which would be unconsciously thrown away as trash.

Cotton balls and other cushioning agents such as wadded paper and rayon, have been a part of pill bottle packaging for over 100 years, and the tradition of stuffing bottles appears to be continuing into the foreseeable future. When you have opened the bottle – after marveling at how much cotton and air you purchased, you should throw away the cotton. Cotton will attract moisture, and moisture is bad for most pills, causing them to stick together and diluting their potency.

FUN FACTS

Before screw-top lids were invented, pill bottles were capped with corks.

Cotton comes off the cotton plant in a ball shape.

People have been using cotton over 7,000 years for various projects; it was first turned into clothing over 5,000 years ago.

PART 5
TECHNOLOGY

Chapter 33

Why do Americans Drive on the Right Side of the Road, but British Drive on the Left?

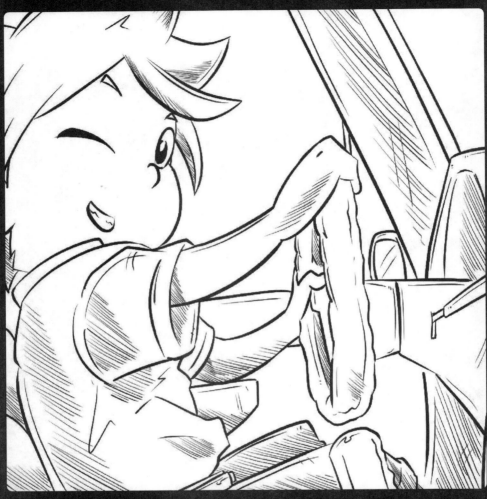

Have you ever seen a rural route U.S. Post Office Jeep? Unlike most cars in the United States, the steering wheel is on the right-hand side so that the carrier can open mailboxes and place the mail inside. If you go to the United Kingdom, you will find that almost all their cars are made that way. Do you know why? It's because they drive on the left side of the road whereas in the United States and the large majority of the world, people drive on the right side. This raises the question, why do people in the United Kingdom prefer to drive on the left side?

A large part of the answer is tradition. Travel used to be a very risky undertaking because the road was full of bandits who lay in wait for an unsuspecting victim. People tended to travel in groups to keep themselves protected, but sometimes a person had to go by oneself. If one did go by oneself, one would take a sword to defend oneself. Since most people were right-handed, it was important to keep the right hand away from the bandits who might jump out. Therefore, travelers would go down the left side of the road.

The British were not the only ones to do this; so did most of the rest of the world – bandits were a problem in all cultures. The British passed this custom on to all its colonies; in fact, most of the places outside the United Kingdom with left-side driving are former British colonies. (Japan was never a British colony, but the British built the railway there and greatly influenced its transportation.) Needless to say, the United States was a British colony, and left side driving of wagons was common at one time in the United States.

As the American Revolution happened in the 1700s, Americans tried to separate themselves from British customs. If the British way was driving on the left side, the American way would be on the right side. Americans had other reasons too for driving their horses and wagons on the right side. For instance, it was much easier to control a wagon from the right side than from the left; similarly, if one were to walk and then board one's horse, one could see oncoming traffic easier walking on the left.

The French too, to prove they were non-British, began driving on the right side. Napoleon Bonaparte spread the custom to all the lands that he conquered; Adolf Hitler did the same when Germany conquered lands in World War II.

In 1967, the British considered legalizing right-side driving, but the resolution did not pass. Since then, the idea of switching has not been seriously considered – just as the idea of switching has not been seriously considered in the United States either.

FUN FACTS

In 2009, Samoa switched from right-side driving to left-side driving so it could import Australian-made cars.

Pennsylvania passed a law in 1792 that stated people using the turnpike had no choice but to travel in the right-hand lane.

Up to 15% of English knights were left-handed, but they too were supposed to drive on the left side.

Chapter 34

Why Are There Interstate Highways in Hawaii?

Let's look at a couple of facts about geography and about language. Fact One, Hawaii is one of the United States; it is a group of islands in the Pacific literally hundreds of miles from the other states. It can only be reached by boat or by plane; you can't drive a car to it from the mainland. Fact Two, the term "inter" means "between others" while "intra" means "within oneself." With those two facts in mind, why do interstate highways exist in Hawaii?

That's right. In case you didn't know, Hawaii has four interstate highways – H-1, H-2, H-3, and H-201. If you know Hawaii geography, H-1 goes from Makaila to Kahala; H-2 stretches from Pearl City to Wahiawa; H-3 goes from Pearl Harbor to Kaneohe; and H-201 runs from Aiea to Honolulu. These are not long highways; H-1 is 27.1 miles, H-2 is 8.3, H-3 is 15.3, and H-201 is 4.1. So, again I ask, why are there interstate highways in Hawaii when they clearly do not go interstate?

The Hawaii interstate highways received their name because they were built as part of The Dwight D. Eisenhower System of Interstate and National Defense Highway. Although they do not connect interstate, they are part of the interstate system. Like interstates on the mainland, the roads are used primarily by civilians, but they are designed for swift troop movement should a national emergency arise.

Other states also have interstate highways that do not actually cross the border into another state. For instance, I-385 in South Carolina stretches from Greenville in the foothills of the Smoky Mountains to Charleston by the seaside.

Interstates have many advantages over traditional highways. For instance, whereas traditional highways have stop lights, most interstates do not. Whereas traditional highways have numerous vehicles traveling at varying speeds from slow tractors to fast cars, on the interstate there are minimum and maximum speed limits. Whereas people can enter and exit the highway at any driveway or side road, the interstate typically has one and off ramps placed at least a mile apart.

FUN FACTS

H-3 is the most expensive interstate to ever be built; it cost $100 million per mile when constructed.

There are over 47,000 miles of interstate highway in the United States.

Because interstates are long and wide, airplanes can land on them in an emergency.

Chapter 35

Why is the Flashing Red Light at the Back of a Train Called "Fred"?

Do you like to watch freight trains go by? My dad loves it. When we are riding with him, he will make it a point to race to the railroad junction so we can see the train go back and count the number of cars. My mom, on the other hand, hates trains; they block the road and keep her away from where she is going.

My dad tells me stories about how every train used to have a caboose. The caboose was the office area; it was also a way to monitor for lost cargo, loose cars, and thieves. He tells of how the conductor used to wave to kids like himself as the train rolled through town.

The caboose served another function as well. On its back hung lanterns. These lanterns helped other trains see that there was something ahead on the tracks at night, and they prevented many accidents. Beginning in the late 1960s and continuing until around 1990, railroads began to do away with cabooses. Because of computers, they no longer needed an office for the conductor, and, because of computer sensors, they no longer needed the brakeman's eyes to verify the status of the cargo. The railroad union and management had agreed that long shifts were no longer required, so the caboose was no longer needed as a motel on wheels. What they still needed, though, was a way to let other trains know that the train was on the track.

In 1969, the Florida East Coast Railway installed a portable flashing rear end device to the train. This red light would flash to let other trains see the end of the train. To reduce costs of hauling around a caboose but yet keep safety high, other railroads began to use them too, installing the device slightly above the coupler on the last car of the train.

The flashing rear end devices gradually began to be called "Fred." At first, they were "flashing rear end devices;" that was shortened to the acronym "F.R.E.D." and soon, instead of people saying, "I have the F-R-E-D," they simply said, "I have Fred."

Some of these end-of-train devices (ETD) not only flashed a warning to other trains, but they also gathered data and sent this data to the engineer's computer, known as the head-of-train device (HTD). Since "Fred" was the name of the rear device, the head-of-train device affectionately became known as Wilma. (Do you remember Fred and Wilma Flintstone, the modern stone age family, who lived in Bedrock? Yabba-dabba-doo if you have heard of this early 1960s cartoon!)

Today's end-of-train devices also help stop a train by applying air pressure to the brake lines of the freight cars. They have a light sensor, so that they run when it is dark – assuming their small generator/battery is charged, and the bulb is not burned out – but not during the day. If you are close to a modern Fred, you will hear it make a beeping sound so that the engineer knows that the rear of the train is in motion.

FUN FACTS

You can purchase a flashing-rear-end-device for your vehicle.

The caboose dates back to the 1830s; it was likely preceded by people doing paperwork in empty boxcars.

Hobby shops have flashing-rear-end devices for model railroad cars for the serious model railroader.

In 1870, approximately 2,700 cabooses were in use on American railroads; by 1900, that number was 17,600.

Chapter 36

Why Are Stop Lights Red and Green Instead of Black and White or Some Other Combination?

When you are really proud of something and want people to notice it, do you set it on your dresser as the centerpiece and then determine what else goes on your dresser based on how it complements your prized possession? I do. The other day, I made a model of an airplane, and then I arranged the other objects on my desk so that they looked good beside it. If you have done something similar, then you can relate to how the colors of the stop light were chosen.

The stop light is designed to show off the color red. Red was chosen because of all the colors, due to its wavelengths, red can be seen the farthest away by the human eye. Red gives people the most time to be able to react.

The creators of the stop light were not the first to notice this trait about red. The first stop light was installed in Cleveland, Ohio on August 15, 1914, and, by the time that this stop light was installed, red was already being used in industrial machinery and by the railroads to alert people of potential danger. Red had a reputation in the culture as representing both high energy and danger, so it was the natural choice for "stop," so red was the obvious choice for the inventors of the stop light to choose.

Since red was to be shown off, the other color(s) that was to represent "go" needed to complement red, not distract from it to make the stop light look offensive; it also needed to be a color that would not blend into red to the point the two were indistinguishable. The railroads had initially adapted white to mean "go" and green to mean "caution." However, using white for "go" resulted in many accidents; the red lens would fall out of a red light, resulting in the red light appearing as white, and trains that were meant to stop plowed into other trains on the track. When white was disbanded as the color for "go," the green light came to mean "go." The railroads eventually did add a third light to represent "caution;" this time they chose yellow, the color that can be seen second best – red is first, remember - by humans from afar.

Just as you choose items that complement what you want to show off, green has been chosen because of how it complements red. If red had not been the first color chosen, then it is unlikely green would have been selected. Because green had already been in use by the railroads, it was economical simply to change the meaning of green from "caution" to "go"

The first stop lights were just red and green. However, because many cars were caught in the intersection when the light changed from red to green, in 1920 yellow debuted between the green and red bulbs to alert motorists that the light was about to change from green to red.

FUN FACTS

The first stop lights were operated manually. When the police officer sitting in the control booth believed that traffic from another direction needed to go, he simply pushed a button.

Some exit signs are now lit in green instead of red, because the red confused people about whether the exit should be taken in an emergency.

The first city with a three-way stop light was Detroit.

Chapter 37

Why Aren't the Letters in Alphabetical Order on a Computer or Typewriter Keyboard?

I don't know about you, but when I was in elementary school, I had to learn my ABC's. I was always taught that they went like this:

A-B-C-D-E-F-G-H-I-J-K-L-M-N-O-P-Q-R-S-T-U-V-W-X-Y-Z

However, whenever I try to type on a keyboard, somebody put them in the wrong order; they go

Q-W-E-R-T-Y-U-I-O-P
A-S-D-F-G-H-J-K-L
and Z-X-C-V-B-N-M

That's crazy! Why can't they be in A-B-C order? I think I would be able to type much faster if they were.

Unbelievably, though, that is exactly why the letters are not in A-B-C order; people would be able to type a lot faster. In fact, where the typewriter was first invented in the 1860s, the keys were in A-B-C order. When the typist pushed down on the letter button, it raised a key which had a letter of type on it. That letter would strike the paper, and then the carriage of the typewriter would move to the left so that the next letter could strike the paper. When the end of the row was reached, the typist would grab the carriage by its hand and pull it all the way to the right and down on click; the typewriter was then ready to start the next line.

Some people, though, were so fast at typing that the keys got jammed. To encourage people to slow down, Christopher Sholes, the inventor of the typewriter. rearranged the alphabet. Upon his friend's advice, he put the letters that are commonly used together in places where they would not tangle up with each other as they headed for the carriage. The keyboard was designed to make the most commonly used letters easy to reach but to be far enough apart from each other that they will not get tangled.

In the 1930s, August Dvorak produced a different keyboard still. Researchers have compared it with the Q-W-E-R-T-Y standard and found that it was no better. Those who were better on it were simply better because of excessive practice. Therefore, Q-W-E-R-T-Y is the keyboard standard used today, whether it is for typewriters, computers, or cell phone texting.

FUN FACTS

The typewriter keyboard is designed so that on the typical word, one letter is taken from the left side and the next letter from the right side.

Thousands of English words can be typed using only the left hand; only a few hundred can be typed using the right hand.

If your computer keyboard is not putting up the right letter and you are sure you are hitting the right letter, be sure your "number lock" is off and that you are set for "English."

The word "typewriter" is the longest English word that can be written using just one row of keys on a keyboard.

Chapter 38

Why is an Error in a Computer Program Called a Bug?

Have you ever left a window open, and the house lights turned on during
or fall? If you have, you probably had some unwanted guests. Moths and ot
attracted to the light, and some will soon be paying you a visit. The moths are I
a dark shelter, and the blackness around a light looks blacker to them than ordina
(Did you ever notice that moths don't land on the light to stay?) Ideally, the dark p
will have heat as well. The inside of a computer is a nice, dark, warm spot – do
more?

On September 9, 1947, the Harvard Mark II, a state-of-the-art compute
Harvard University in Cambridge, Massachusetts for the U.S. Navy, made an err
to say, computers are not known for making errors. Granted, if the operator
typographical error or has given poorly worded commands then the computer wil

the answers that it should, but the computing process itself is perfect. On this particular day, though, the correct data had been entered and the computer produced the wrong answer.

Grace Hopper, one of the attendants, was as perplexed as anyone. After all, computers may be complicated, but they are simply a series of gears that grind as told, and therefore should always have the right answer. Having verified that the data had been entered correctly and that the answer was indeed incorrect, she concluded that it had to be a hardware problem; that is, one of the gears did not turn as it was designed to do. She checked the computer and found a dead moth that had been trapped under a gear. She exclaimed, "I found the bug!" (Now, whether it was literally her that did it is a matter of debate. Some scholars point out that she may have gotten the credit, but someone else may have actually done it; just like we claim that Napoleon found the Rosetta Stone when it was really his soldiers.)

The moth, a butterfly-like creature with a two-inch (five centimeter) wingspan is on display today at the Smithsonian Museum in Washington, D.C. Ever since that day, when a computer does not function as it is supposed to, people say that it needs to be "debugged."

FUN FACTS

The first recorded use of the term "bug" associated with electronics was in a letter by Thomas Edison in 1890.

The typical human brain is superior to the very best computer.

Grace Hopper became one of the inventors of the programming language COBOL.

Chapter 39

Why are Pencils in the U.S. Yellow?

Grab a pencil, please.

Now take a look at it. What color is it? If you live in the United States, it is likely yellow. Almost all pencils in the United States are yellow.

The first thing to realize is that pencils do not have to be yellow. Although yellow is by far the most popular color for a pencil in the United States, it is not the most popular color in other countries. In Brazil pencils are generally green; the same is true with Germany. In Southern Europe, most pencils are dark red or black with yellow stripes. Pencils tend to be red with black bands in Australia.   So why are they yellow in the United States?

The influx of yellow pencils began over 120 years ago. At the World's Fair in 1889, Koh-I-Noor, an Austro-Hungarian pencil company, introduced the yellow pencil. Their yellow color was designed to suggest luxury, just like yellow diamonds do, and the pencil was supposedly made from the best graphite China had to offer. The gimmick was a marketing hit, and soon other companies were also making pencils that were yellow to indicate quality (and to muscle in on Koh-I-Noor's market).

Did you notice that I said, "the best graphite China had to offer"? Today's "lead pencils" do not have lead. They have graphite. Graphite is preferred because it resists aging, moisture, and ultraviolet rays.

Notice the shape of your pencil. I'm guessing that it is hexagonal; most pencils are. The hexagon-shape is to keep the pencil from rolling off your writing surface. The hexagon-shape also makes it easier to grip. Don't think that the pencil companies created the hexagon-shape with just the consumer in mind – by using less wood the pencil company saves considerable money.

What is the number of your pencil? I'm guessing it is number two. The number refers to the softness of the graphite; the larger the number, the harder the graphite is and the lighter the marks are on the paper. If the lead is too soft, the lead will break, and if the lead is too hard, it will not mark well. The number two is the most common – number two is number one in this case – because it is the perfect lead for writing everyday messages.

Most people take for granted that pencils should be yellow, hexagonal, and have number two lead; they don't think a thing about it. It is important to realize that it doesn't have to be that way, and in many places in the world it is not. What you have in front of you is a well thought out invention, and the world would be a very different place without it.

FUN FACTS

Drafters, designers, and engineers generally prefer #3 pencils.

John Steinbeck, the author of the *Grapes of Wrath*, went through sixty sharpened pencils per day while writing his novel.

The first pencils made in the United States were blue, not yellow.

Chapter 40

Why Do We Sleep on Pillows?

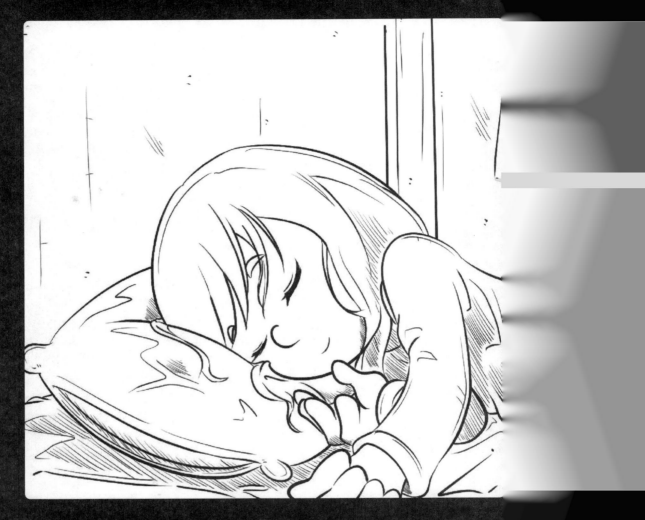

My dad is a napper. Each night after supper, he will lie down on the floor to one of us kids, "Hand me a pillow. I'm going to take a quick nap."

"Hand me a pillow?" I had never thought about it until the other day, but the occurred to me, "Why do people insist on a pillow prior to going to sleep?" I unde needing a teddy bear, but does an adult need a pillow? Why don't we just lay on cup our hands to make a pillow when we sleep on our sides?

The concept of the pillow dates back to Mesopotamia – modern-day Iraq ago. Ancient people didn't grab pillows; they grabbed rocks. While the rock hel head, that was not the primary reason people originally started taking something – they took the rock so the bugs could not get into their ears, nose, and mouth as they slept on the ground

In ancient Egypt, it wasn't just bugs they were worried about entering one's head – they feared evil spirits. Pillows there were made out of carved stone, wood, ivory, and marble and images to scare off bad spirits were carved into them; the pillow became a decorative piece.

Having a pillow was a symbol of luxury until the Industrial Revolution. Pillows became more affordable, and people of all classes could afford them. Pillows also moved from the bedroom into other rooms in the house, such as becoming couch decorations. Today, pillows come in a variety of shapes and sizes, and they are made from numerous materials. The cloth of the pillowcase itself will yellow and turn brown, though, so if you don't have protectors around your pillow, you will likely want to replace them every couple of years.

FUN FACTS

Wealthy people in Greece and Rome during the Greek and Roman Empires were the first to use feather pillows.

Although the technology was there to make a soft pillow prior to the Greek Empire, no one did – hard pillows were thought to be better for the body; i.e., soft pillows were thought to steal energy.

More pillows are used for decorating than sleeping today.

Chapter 41

Why Are Doorknobs So Far from the Hinges?

Doors are the end of one thing and the beginning of something else; doors can also be a barrier – for good or bad – between two things. Doors are gateways between worlds, and therefore past generations have associated superstition with the doorway. Doorknobs give us control over the door; they give us control over our destiny. We can decide whether to turn it or not. It's not just the concept of turning it that fascinates me; it's the doorknob's placement? Have you ever wondered why the doorknob is placed so far away from the door hinges? Does this placement have to do with superstition or with science?

If you are at school right now, I want you to go outside to the teeter-totters (see-saw) on the playground. Go stand in the middle of the teeter-totter (see-saw) and try to make the teeter-totter (see-saw) go up and down. (If you can't get to a teeter-totter (see-saw), at least try to do it in your mind.) It is hard to move the teeter-totter (see-saw). Now, go stand at the end of the teeter-totter (see-saw) where the bench is in the air. You may have to jump a bit to reach it but try to make the end move now. Chances are you made the end move with ease.

That is the simple science behind doors. The doorknob is placed far from the hinges because that distance makes it easy for us to swing the door. If the doorknob were right beside the hinges, we could not swing the door with ease on its hinges. It is science, not superstition, which explains the placement of the doorknob.

The doorknob is a fairly new invention, but the concept of doors dates back to ancient times. Early doors were nothing more than an animal skin or a slab of wood between rooms. (I've been in a few houses where people have beads dangling from the doorway.) Although humans are social animals, throughout history, people have always needed "me" time, and have tried to isolate themselves from the world.

The pin-and-tumbler technology needed to make door locks was developed around 3000 B.C.E. in Egypt. The hinges we use on doors today were first used in the Greek Empire. During the Roman Empire, Romans invented the sliding door. The first doorknob-like object was a mere piece of leather attached to the door to run a string through, so they could tie the door closed. People could also bolt the door from the inside to keep out unwanted people.

In 1878, the first doorknob with an internal locking mechanism was patented. With the Industrial Revolution, prices fell so that the average person could afford doors with doorknobs. At this time, too, doorknobs went from being merely functional to also being decorative. Door levers – a doorknob with a long stick on it – began in the Tudor period but became mainstream in the 1900s. The lever provides a way to open doors for those who cannot turn a doorknob.

The doorknob gives us control over our world. Do we stay where we are? Do we open the door and see what is inside, perhaps releasing what is inside into where we are? Do we dare to go through the door? With the doorknob, we are in control.

FUN FACTS

Most doors swing inward.
When given a choice of push or pull when entering a room, "push" will usually be the right choice.

The world's largest door stands 465 feet high; it is at the Kennedy Space Center in Florida.

The revolving door was patented in 1888.

Chapter 42

Why Do Some Electrical Lamp Plugs Have Two Prongs, but Others Have Three?

If you have a choice between using an electronic gadget with a two-prong plug or one with a three-prong plug, which should you choose? My gut reaction was to use one with two prongs, because it would fit in either a two-prong or a three-prong outlet. My mom never let me do that, though, because she thought the third prong helped the plug to stay in the outlet socket better. I have to admit, my mom was right – If you have a choice between using a gadget with two prongs or one with three prongs, always get the one with three prongs.

My mom was right when she said that a third prong helped to keep the plug inserted; however, there is a much better reason for using a third prong. If you know anything about electricity, you know that the first prong brings electricity to the device and the second takes electricity from the device. The third prong, though, helps in case of an overload.

The third prong has its roots in the work of Benjamin Franklin, the man who invented the lightning rod in the 1700s. The lightning rod would take a burst of electricity and route it safely into the ground where it could not hurt anyone or anything. Likewise, if lightning were to strike a device without a third prong that was plugged into the power system, the device would be ruined from the power spike. When my dad was growing up, people would unplug their televisions and VCRs to prevent a power spike from ruining their devices. Today, if a sudden spike does get into your system, the third prong takes away that extra power and directs it into the ground, preventing damaged electronics, fires, and electric shocks. It is called an 'earth' because it takes the electricity to earth (it generally has a yellow and green wire; whereas the live wire is brown, and the neutral blue).

Two-prong plugs have been around since residential electricity became common in the 1880s. These early lights generally hung from ceiling light sockets. In 1904, the wall socket began to become popular. The three-prong plug was invented in 1927. Today, many building codes insist on three prongs in new buildings. Three-prong plugs are definitely much safer, so, if given a choice, always use items with three-prongs.

FUN FACTS

Electricity is incredibly fast – it travels at 186,000 miles per second.

The toaster, sewing machine, fan, and kettle were the first home appliances to be powered by electricity.

The majority of today's electricity is generated by burning coal.

Chapter 43
Why Do Men's Shirts Button Differently Than Women's Shirts?

When my grandma came to babysit my sister and I, we would play "Hide the Button." It is a game similar to "Hide and Seek" but the hider hides the button instead of one's body. (My grandma couldn't move to hide too well, nor could she stand for too long, so "Hide the Button" had all of the elements of Hide and Seek except for having to hide.) Once the button was hidden, the seekers would start searching for it. The hider would call, "warm . . . getting hotter" as someone got near it, and, if they drifted from it, would call, "getting cool . . . getting colder . . . getting colder still." Once someone had found the button, it was their turn to hide it.

When grandma got too tired to walk around, we would simply call out a place in the room and be told that we were either "hot" or "cold." In that game, we treated the button like it was a common everyday object – which it was. However, that was not always the case for buttons. Prior to the Industrial Revolution, only the very rich had buttons.

The ancestor of the button was likely invented when clothing was invented, those loincloths needed to be decorated. The oldest button-like object, a flat shell, dates back over 5,000 years to where Pakistan is today.

The button as we know it as a fastener was invented in the Middle Ages in Western Europe. The first clothing with buttonholes appeared in Germany around 1200, and France soon had a button-maker's guild. Buttons in the Middle Ages were designed for two things – function and status. Only the rich could afford buttoned clothing. In those days, a rich man needed to be able to hold a weapon in their right-hand while being able to button or unbutton their shirt, so the buttons were put on the right. Meanwhile, rich women could afford having servants to dress them, and so to make it easier on the servants, the buttons were put on the left. The buttons on clothing were designed to accent the body's natural shape, and the buttons themselves were often very gaudy.

Today, men's shirts still have buttons on the right and women's shirts have them on the left. Even though buttons have become mainstream, a good button shirt is still considered formal wear. Some fashions change yearly, but others, such as button shirts, have an 800-plus year tradition.

FUN FACTS

Today's buttons are primarily made of plastic, but in the past buttons were primarily made from seashells, wood, horns, bones, and metal.

Buttons are often measured in lignes (this measures the diameter of the button); 40 lignes equals one inch (2.54 centimeters).

Although buttons are over 5000 years old, the buttonhole is only slightly over 800 years old.

Chapter 44

Why Do Traditional Combs Have Two Sets of Teeth?

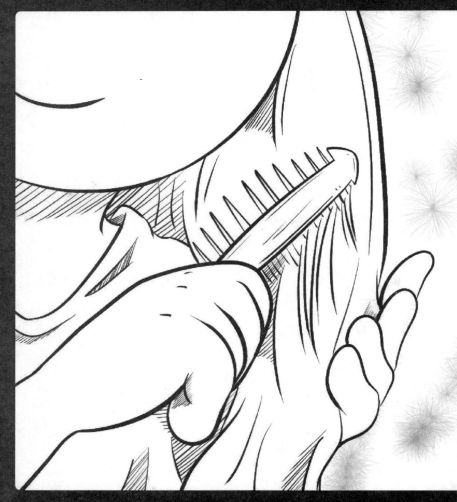

Long before people were farmers, they were hunters and gatherers. That is lived off the land, eating from bushes and trees where they were in season whatever animals they could. They were nomads, traveling from place to place food.

It shouldn't surprise you, then, to learn that the plow was not the first signific of people. A case, though, can be made that the comb was. Combs have been earliest of civilization in Egypt, Sudan, and Persia. They were used as decoration and eventually evolved into a way to untangle and organize the hair.

The traditional comb has two sets of teeth, a fine set that are close together and a second set that are further apart. This type of comb, which many people still use today, has been found at Egyptian excavation sites. These combs were made from wood, rubber, bone, silver, gold, and tortoiseshell. Today's combs are often made of nylon.

The comb was two devices in one. The fine set of teeth was used to remove lice and lice eggs. (Yes, lice have been a problem since the earliest of time.) The other set of teeth was used to remove tangles.

If you run a comb through your hair, it tends to make the hair lay down. It took over 4000 years, but people eventually invented the brush. The earliest brushes, invented around 1777, had a tooth here and there. The air flow between the teeth allowed the hair to maintain its fluff.

Today, numerous styles of brushes and combs are available. The traditional comb is still popular, though, even if the majority of people do not realize what the second set of teeth is for.

FUN FACTS

When you comb your hair, you activate the sebum glands, the glands that help oil your hair. (If done a couple of times per day – but no more - this leads to healthy hair.)

Combs have been used as musical instruments in which the musician picked the spokes.

The spokes on a comb are called "teeth."

Never share a comb. (Combs still pull-out lice eggs, and you may unwittingly get an infestation.)

Chapter 45

Why Do Horses Wear Shoes But Cows Don't?

At the farm the other day, I saw pigs, chickens, cows, and horses. All the other animals were walking around on the same grass, and yet the horse had shoes. I couldn't help asking myself, why the horse got shoes, but the pigs, chickens, and cows did not. It raised the question, why do horses need shoes?

By shoes, I am not referring to dress shoes or sneakers like you and I wear. Although horses have worn booties in the past, today's horseshoe is a U-shape piece of steel or aluminum that fits around the horse's hoof. Just as you and I need to try on shoes to make sure they fit; the blacksmith will make sure the horse has proper fitting shoes. Also, just like some people need extra support, if a horse needs extra support, special shoes can be constructed for special needs. Whereas our shoes are either tied to our feet or are so snug they won't fall off, the horse's shoes are nailed to its feet. (Don't worry, the horse is not in any pain.) Just like it is important for you and I to have shoes that fit well, the same is true for horses.

Believe it or not, horses wear shoes for the same reasons that you and I wear shoes – it hurts their feet to walk on the ground. I remember when my mom used to drop me in a gravel parking lot to go swimming. Those rocks hurt my feet, and I walked very slowly and carefully to minimize the pain. Horses have the same sensations in their feet as I had in mine. Granted, some breeds of horses are more tender footed than others, but all can walk faster and with more confidence if they have on shoes.

It's not just pain that inspires horse owners to shoe their horses. When a horse is going on jagged terrain, there is a real possibility the horse might cut itself. The shoes help protect the horse (and ensures the rider still has transportation). Besides protecting the horse's foot from injury, the horseshoe also prevents sickness such as ringworm from spreading. You and I don't like to walk on injuries and sore spots, and neither does a horse. Horseshoes enable the horse to feel secure.

Wild horses don't wear shoes, but wild horses also aren't carrying the weight of a human being (or two) on their backs nor are they dragging a plow. Horse's hooves were not meant to be carrying people, and therefore the shoe helps protect the hooves from wearing down as the horse works in partnership with people.

FUN FACTS

The horseshoe was invented around 400 B.C.E.

The first horseshoes were made of plants, rawhide, and scraps of leather.

For a horseshoe to be lucky, it needs to be turned up like this "U," so the luck doesn't fall out.

The devil is often pictured as a cloven animal who does not want nails placed into him; therefore, a horseshoe became a symbol of keeping away evil spirits around 900 C.E

Chapter 46

Why Do Birds Fly into Windows?

Have you ever seen a two-way mirror? Police have them in their rooms where the witness picks out the crook; the crook can't see the witness, but the witness can see the crook. Daycares and many stores have them so that parents and security guards can see what is happening but so that the people being watched cannot see them. If you have been on either side of a one-way mirror, then you can better understand why birds fly into windows.

Have you ever heard a bird fly into a window? The bird usually hits it with a hard "Bonk!" The noise is enough to scare someone into thinking an intruder is trying to enter the home. In many cases, the birds hit so hard, they knock themselves unconscious. Sometimes birds that live through it are often physically hurt, and either die from their injuries or become easy prey because of their injuries. Other times birds can manage to recover and fly off.

What you are seeing through your window is very different from what the bird is seeing. During the day, the bird is not seeing a glass; it perceives that it can fly straight. What it does see – a houseplant which it would like to eat, a reflection of everything that is behind it, or the reflection of itself that it perceives is a rival bird – is enough to make the bird want to swoop through the hole it perceives to be existing. Birds are very headstrong – no pun intended, so don't be surprised if the bird will likely keep trying to eat that plant/roost in that tree/scare off that rival bird, knocking into the window repeatedly until it has knocked itself out.

If you have ever heard a "Bonk! Bonk! Bonk!" on your window, it was probably on a foggy night. Birds were likely migrating and saw a light in your home. Again, the birds can't see the glass, and, in the fog, they mistook the light for a star that they were trying to follow. When the lead bird crashed head-first into the glass, some of those behind it made the same mistake.

To stop birds from flying into your windows, consider adding curtains so that the birds cannot see the lights through them at night. To prevent them from trying to fly through them during the day, place stickers on them every few inches so the bird realizes it is not a big hole. Screens also help, hiding the plants from the birds, cutting down on reflections, and making a grid across the glass so the bird realizes it cannot get through.

FUN FACTS

Over 365 million to 1 billion birds die annually by injuries resulting from running head-first into windows.

The average U.S. home has eight windows.

The first glass window was made in Egypt 100 A.D.

PART 6

QUESTIONS MOST PEOPLE ARE TOO POLITE TO ASK...

BUT WOULD REALLY LIKE ANSWERED

Chapter 47

Why Do Birds Poo-Poo on Cars?

Have you ever seen a cartoon in which birds are sitting on a branch or a telephone wire and one says to the other, "Look! That guy just waxed his car. Let's dive-bomb it"? Have you ever wondered if birds actually do target cars?

Unbelievably, the answer is yes – but it is not because they hate you. Birds are attracted to cars because they can see their reflections just as you and I do if we look into a mirror. The bird believes it is another bird and starts to fly toward it. Upon getting closer, the bird may realize it is just a reflection, but now the reflecting metal looks like water. Birds like to poop on water so that predators cannot track them, so, seeing a restroom, they take advantage. (My grandma is the same way – if there is a restroom, she likes to take advantage of it.)

Red and blue cars are the most likely targets. Even if the bird doesn't see its reflection in a red car, the color red makes the bird think it is seeing a cluster of berries, and so it will fly down to explore. Blue, meanwhile, reminds the bird of lake waters, and as mentioned previously, birds like to poop over water. Silver cars, meanwhile, repel birds and are very scary to birds, but birds poo-poo when scared, so silver cars get hit a lot too. Clean cars are more likely to be targets than dirty cars because birds can see their reflections in clean cars.

To be honest, birds are putting more than poo-poo on your car. Whereas ostriches have the ability to do #1 and #2 separately, most birds do not. Instead, everything just comes out of one place, so that white soupy mix is actually both pee and poop. These droppings are more than just an eyesore – they contain uric acid, a substance that is bad for your car's metal.

Birds of a feather do flock together, and if your car is parked under a spot where the birds are likely to gather, it is much more likely to get splattered on. Birds tend to gather in trees, on wires, and on roof edges; therefore, if you park under a tree, under a wire, or near a building, your vehicle is much more likely to get struck than if you parked it away from these.

You can also decrease the odds of a bird leaving its calling card by putting a rubber snake on your car. Birds recognize the snake as a predator and will stay away from it. They will also be less attracted to your car if you cover the mirrors so they cannot see their reflections. A third way is to put a covering over your car.

FUN FACTS

Birds are least attracted to green cars.

Different birds are attracted to different colors of cars; a cardinal bird will be attracted to a red car while a meadowlark will prefer a yellow car. (The car helps serve as camouflage.)

Shedding poo-poo is one way that birds make themselves lighter to fly.

Birds poo-poo on things to mark their territory.

Chapter 48

Why is Pee "#1" and Poo-Poo "#2"?

Have you ever seen an usually small person and called excitedly to your parents, "Mom, dad, look at the midget"? You likely barely finished your sentence before your mom said, "Hush! It's not polite to call someone a 'midget'". You quickly learned that you could use words such as "short" or "small" but that the term "midget" was offensive.

Many people are not comfortable using certain words, and they prefer to speak in euphemisms, words that do not sound as harsh but convey the same meaning. Bodily functions such as going to pee and poo-poo are two of the things that they do not like to speak of, but, sometimes in society, they must be said. For instance, if you are watching a movie at the movie theater and need to pee, you need to be able to communicate that to your mom. If you simply announce, "I need to pee," your mom will be embarrassed, so you must find a better way.

"I need to use the restroom" is a very polite, socially acceptable way of saying, "I have got to go pee." However, that leaves some questions unanswered. Because it takes longer to poo-poo than pee, your parents and teachers may ask you for more specific details, so they know how long to plan for you to be gone.

Many families, schools, churches, day cares, and other social establishments have created the code of "#1 for pee" and "#2 for poo-poo". Just by holding up a finger, you can let your parents know why you need to visit the restroom. How did this code come about?

It may have begun at the one-room schoolhouse. A student could discreetly put his hand up and flash the teacher one finger or two fingers. The teacher would nod approvingly, and the student could slip out, unnoticed by almost everyone. Not a single word had to be exchanged, and the lesson could keep being taught.

Although any numbers could have been selected, when teachers originally taught the system, they likely pointed down for "one" and toward the back for "two." Also, "poo" rhymes with "two" so it made sense that "poo-poo" be given number two. If "poo" was two, then it made sense that "pee" should be "one" or "three;" "one" because it comes before two and "three" because it rhymes with "pee." Over time, one became the symbol of choice.

I have read other theories about how the 1-2 Code came about. Some of these theories I know are simply not true. For instance, I read the 1-2 Code came about because it took one flush for pee and two for poo-poo, but the 1-2 Code system was established in the days of the outhouse long before flush toilets became available. Others make just enough sense that they can't be ruled out. For instance, one theory claims that "1" looks like a boy standing to pee and a "2" looks like a boy sitting on a toilet with his pants on the floor. Nobody knows for sure how the code happened, but all agree it is certainly widely used today.

FUN FACTS

Ancient Roman spies used urine as invisible ink; it was invisible until heated.

Males urinate faster than females until around the age of 50, and then men slow down.

Poop is made of 75% water.

Chapter 49

Why Do Some Campers Pee on Their Campfire?

Have you ever gone camping? If so, you probably experienced a campfire. The campfire is something that most people gather around for light and warmth. It is also used for cooking. Have you ever noticed how most people let the fire smolder overnight and then, the next morning, the campers – at least the men – pee on the campfire as it is time to leave. It's amazing how "camping" becomes "camp peein'".

If this tradition grosses you out, you are probably wondering why people who are normally so civilized could be so uncouth. There are three reasons that I know of for this behavior, and they range from practical to instinctual.

The most practical reason is to make sure the fire is out. No one wants to leave a spark that would create a forest fire. Most people who pee on the campfire use peeing as one of several ways to put the fire out. Pouring water over it is by far the best way, but sometimes water is not available. Therefore, water, soil, and urine can all be used to deprive the fire of oxygen. Most campers truly love the environment, and they want to preserve it. Peeing on the campfire is not a sign of disrespect for nature.

The second practical reason is that most people like to solve a problem in the easiest way possible. To say people are lazy is to put things rudely; most people perceive themselves as working smarter, not harder. In front of them they see a campfire that they need to make sure is put out and inside them they have a bladder that needs to be emptied. The easiest way to resolve both problems is to empty the bladder onto the campfire.

The third reason is instinct. If you have a male dog that is not neutered, it probably pees on almost everything when you take it on a walk. Dogs like to mark their territory. If a dog senses another dog has peed in a spot previously, the dog will pee there to make sure it has the top pee. Humans, too, are born with a competitive instinct. When humans pee on the fire, they are marking their territory. (I don't know about you, but I'm not likely to touch a log that someone has peed on.)

Peeing should not be relied on to put out a fire. Even if you guzzled drinks all night long, you likely won't have enough fluid to put out a fire. If the fire is hot, your pee will quickly turn to steam. (Have you ever smelled hot urine mixed with smoke? I wonder why a candle-company hasn't tried to replicate that smell?) Be aware that urine splashes may bounce off logs and bounce back onto you. peeing on the campfire may be a family tradition, but care and common sense need to be utilized when doing it. Also, keep in mind who you are camping with; some people would lose total respect for you if you do it. NEVER pee in front of little children. Remember your manners, and respect those around you as well as the environment.

FUN FACTS

Campfires come in many forms; the tee-pee shape and the log-cabin are the most popular.

A campfire can get as hot as 900 degrees Fahrenheit (480 Celsius).

Birch wood burns quickly; oak wood burns slowly.

Chapter 50
Why Do Boogers Taste Salty?

Stop me if you have heard this joke: What's the difference between boogers and broccoli? Answer: Kids won't eat broccoli.

Do you eat your boogers?

Of course not. No one I have ever met claims to have eaten their boogers. Yet, somehow, almost everyone knows that boogers are salty.

Well, would it make you feel better if I admitted that I had done it? I'm a curious person and I wanted to see for myself how they tasted. Having tried one, I admit that it was very salty. (I don't encourage you to try one, but I suspect you probably already have.)

Boogers are the pieces of rubber-like mucus that is occasionally found inside one's nose. If you have never heard of the term "booger," perhaps you have heard them called "stuffies." They literally stuff the nose and make it hard to breathe. (Believe it or not, there is no scientific name for them.) Although they may be a nuisance when they clog our nasal

passageways, boogers are actually helping us by keeping unwanted germs, dust, and dirt from entering our body.

Boogers are pieces of mucus that were formed in the nostrils and sinus passages that have caught some dust and dirt. They are being moved outward by those little hairs in your nose, the cilia; the boogers are on a slow-moving conveyor belt. Snot is designed to be sticky and rubbery, and the dust and dirt it has collected gives it shape.

Your body relies on electro chemicals, and salt is released as a byproduct. Sweat and tears – as well as boogers – have a salty taste because of this. That salt you are tasting is something that came from within your own body.

Are boogers good to eat? I put one on my tongue to try it, and it was so salty I didn't have the desire to keep it in my mouth any longer – or maybe I was just grossed out because it was a booger. I have seen kids eat their boogers and they have no side effects, but do you really want all that mucus, dirt, and dust in your body? Your body is rejecting it by pushing it out through the nose; putting it back into your body is not the wisest thing to do.

Boogers are not a great source of nutrition, but they do have some nutritional value. In general, the typical booger has twenty calories, and contains sodium, iron, proteins, and Vitamin C. Boogers have germ-killing bacteria in them, and therefore can actually help freshen one's mouth by killing harmful bacteria in it. The literature is very mixed about whether boogers are good for you; therefore, because they are not socially acceptable to consume, I would not eat them.

It's best not to pick boogers. If you have a booger that is ready to be released, grab a tissue, and blow the booger into it. If you put your finger in your nose, you may be getting germs from your finger into your nose. Also, you will get germs from your nose onto your fingers. Not only is it germy, but it can become a habit, and most people think it is gross if they see you picking your nose in public – and especially gross if you eat what you have picked – even though they themselves have likely done the exact same thing in the past.

FUN FACTS

A flu germ can live inside a booger for 24 hours.

A sick person can produce a liter of mucus per day.

The cilia – nose hairs – move mucus in two directions – to the back of the throat or to the end of the nose.

Chapter 51

Why Do Boogers Stick to the Wall?

I like to think that I was a good kid when I was a child, but I remember laying in my bed at night running a booger between my finger and the wall. I was supposed to be sleeping, but I was bored. The booger reminded me of Play-Doh; except it was rubbery.

I was a budding scientist – or a gross kid, one or the other. As I moved the booger around, I eventually noticed that it collected so much dust and dirt that it lost its stickiness. I also noticed that the more I rolled it, the darker it became.

Boogers are made of mucus; stuff that our nasal passages generate to keep the nose and throat lubricated. Even when we are healthy, we generate mucus. When we are ill or in an area with lots of dust and pollen, our mucus has to get serious about keeping the lungs free of dirt. The typical booger consists of water and mucin. Mucin is the sticky substance that catches incoming germs, dirt, and dust. As it catches these, it often becomes the color of the item it is catching. Thus, if you are standing in a fire breathing ashes, your booger is probably going to come out black.

The color of your boogers also provides a clue about what is happening in your nose and in your body as a whole. For instance, if you have green or dark yellow boogers, it is evidence that white-blood cells are fighting off a virus. If you have a red booger, you likely have a cracked mucus membrane. (This is not a serious medical issue, but should the bleeding persist for hours, or the red boogers keep appearing for days, you may want to get it checked out.) Although these are the most common colors of boogers, boogers can be any color depending on what your mucus has come into contact with.

Boogers are hardened mucus, but the mucus is not so hard that it simply peels off your nose. As air rolls through your nostrils, it dries the mucus that is inside the nostrils. If you are in a room with a dehumidifier or a dry climate, you are more likely to have boogers because the moisture is being removed from the mucus.

The mucus, though, is not completely dry in a booger, and therefore that stickiness will allow the booger to stick to the wall. If you come back to your masterpiece a few days later, you will notice that it is likely still stuck on the wall but that it has shrunk in size because the remaining moisture has evaporated from it.

FUN FACTS

Boogers can be found in the intestines as well as in the nose.

Boogers that are airborne by sneezes can travel at speeds of 100 miles per hour.

25% of people pick their nose at least once per day; 20% pick their nose five or more times per day.

Chapter 52
Why Do Beans and Broccoli Make Me Fart More Than Other Foods?

Pff!

    My friends and I were having a debate the other day, and maybe you have an opinion about this too: Is the nursery rhyme "Beans, Beans, the Magical Fruit" or "Beans, Beans, the Musical Fruit"?

    Whether beans are "magical" or "musical," we can all agree that beans certainly produce some bodily noises – and sometimes smells. Have you ever wondered what beans contain that most foods don't that give beans this magical, musical ability?

    The scientific answer is oligosaccharides, natural sugars. These sugar molecules are so big that they pass right through the stomach and the small intestine, and it is up to the large intestine to break them down. When the bacteria in the large intestine breaks these down, it produces methane, carbon dioxide, and hydrogen. It takes longer to break down high fiber foods, and, because they must remain in the intestine longer, high fiber foods have more time to ferment than most foods. High fiber foods contain sulfur, and that sulfur is what you are smelling.

Believe it or not, people fart a lot – and most are not smelly. Many farts are simply trapped air finding freedom. Only 1% of farts smell – but, boy, does that 1% smell!

Beans are not the only food that will cause you to produce smelly farts. Beans are legumes, and other legumes, such as lentils, chickpeas, peas, and peanuts, will also make you pass an excessive amount of terrible-smelling gas. Don't let this stop you from eating them. These foods are an excellent source of fiber and can help you grow healthy intestinal bacteria, decrease blood sugar, and lower bad cholesterol.

Legumes are not the only foods that will make your farts smell terrible. Broccoli, cabbage, and asparagus will make your farts smell like rotten eggs. Foods such as milk, yogurt, apples, and pears will cause many – but not all - people to release gaseous odors. Unbelievably, food is not the only reason for smelly farts. If you have a food intolerance, food that is normally broken down by most people in the stomach will travel to your large intestine where the bacteria there will break it down and release sulfur as a byproduct. Some medications also have the side effect of producing smelly gas. For instance, antibiotics often kill bad bacteria, but they also can kill the good bacteria in the intestine, and without these good bacteria to help break things down your gas is going to smell. A fourth cause of smelly farts is too many bacteria in the digestive system. Another popular reason for smelly farts is constipation when something is stuck in the colon and gas passes over it.

If you are embarrassed about the number of smelly farts you have, consider changing your diet so you avoid an excess of high fiber foods. For the foods you do eat, eat slowly and chew thoroughly to enhance the digestion process. Drink more water and eat more yogurt; this will lubricate your system and produce the good kind of bacteria that will aid in digestion. Make sure it is water, though; carbonated beverages such as soda have gas inside them.

FUN FACTS

The average person farts between 15-25 times per day.

People fart more when sleeping than when awake.

Over 700 species of bacteria call your large intestine home.

Chapter 53

Why Are Public Toilet Seats U-Shaped but Most Residential Toilet Seats Are O-Shaped?

When you clean up from dinner and put the salad dressings and such away, have you ever accidently tried to put the wrong lid on something? At first it looked like it would fit, but, when you set it on the bottle, you realized that the lid belonged to another bottle. If you have ever done that, then you can probably understand at least one of the reasons public toilet seats are U-shaped while most residential toilet seats are O-shaped.

Thieves will steal anything that they can use or resell. Thieves do steal toilet paper; that's why it is often kept locked in a dispenser so that only one roll can be seen at a time. If the roll were left out where the public could take it, somebody would. It makes sense then, that thieves would steal toilet seats too. However, because the public toilet seat is designed so that it will not fit onto residential toilets – just as the lids from the bottles may look interchangeable but are not, the public toilet seat is of no value to a thief.

A second economic reason businesses go with the U shape is that it is cheaper to make. Because the part that would join the circles at the top is cut out, that amount of material is saved on each toilet seat. That saving is passed on to the business.

The public toilet is U-shaped for hygiene reasons as well. One, you will notice that you can lift up on the lip of the edge on the public toilet. Two, the front of one's body does not rub where the front of someone else's body has been. Both of these make the U much more sanitary.

At home, your parents likely have a toilet that is designed for them. The public toilet, though, has to be one-size fits all. The cutout portion of the U meanwhile allows people to sit at ease regardless of one's build. The U-shape also dispenses the person's weight better; an O-shape seat is much more likely to break if excess weight is on it than a U-shaped seat.

Sometimes businesses don't have a choice between U-shaped or O-shaped toilet seats. Many cities have laws in place regarding public restrooms, and they have opted for the U-shaped toilets. Beginning in 1955, plumbers' unions have mandated that their members install U-shaped toilet seats in public restrooms, and if contractors or business professionals are using union labor, they have to use the U-shaped lids.

FUN FACTS

The toilet seat is the cleanest part of a typical public bathroom. (It's because everyone makes sure it is clean before they sit on it.)

More people have cellphones than have modern plumbing.

The typical computer keyboard has 200 times more germs than a typical toilet seat.

Chapter 54

Why is My Pee Usually Light Yellow, but Sometimes It's a Different Color?

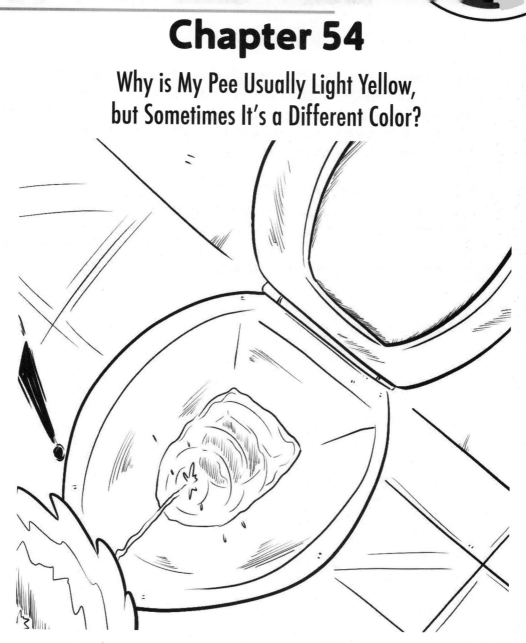

Have you ever checked the motor oil of a car? To check it on most cars, you must remove the dipstick, wipe it off, reinsert it, and pull it out again. When you look at the oil on a dipstick, it is important to make sure the oil level is where it needs to be and to look at the color of the oil. The color tells a lot about the health of the oil and of the engine. If the color is light brown, the oil is new. If the oil is solid black, it needs to be changed. If it has silver in it, your engine needs a repair.

Your pee works in a very similar way. The color of your pee tells you about how your body is functioning. The ideal color for pee is a light yellow. The tinge of yellow is the waste product.

If your pee is clear, then you are drinking too much fluid; that is, the water in your system is not mixing with any waste product. On the other hand, if your pee is a dark yellow or orange, you are either not drinking enough or are consuming a lot of B-12 or Vitamin C.

The color of your pee can also be influenced by the foods you eat. Sometimes your pee can be dyed by the foods you eat. For instance, if you have beets, rhubarb, or blueberries, you may pee pink or even red. Blue and green pee is not found in nature, but it could occur if you ate or drank something that had those food colors in it, such as a striped candy-cane or a St. Patrick's Day green beverage. Medications can also change your pee's color.

If your pee is too light, try to drink less fluids. If your pee is too dark, try to drink more. If your pee is a color other than these, quit eating the foods likely causing the pee to be that color and see if your urine gets the dye out of your system and goes back to a light-yellow color. If your pee remains the unusual color even though you are no longer consuming foods with natural dyes (beets) or man-made dyes (green soda), ask a doctor for advice.

FUN FACTS

The average person pees between six or seven times per day.

People who drink beverages with caffeine, such as coffee, tea, and soda, must pee more than people who drink pure water.

It is normal for a senior adult to get up twice in the night to go and pee.

Chapter 55

Why Does Some Poo-Poo Float But Most Poo-Poo Sinks?

I don't know about you, but most people look down in the toilet bowl when they are done to see what kind of a masterpiece they have left behind. The view in the toilet is much like the view of a kaleidoscope; it is always different but always interesting.

If you do look, you have probably noticed that most poo-poo falls to the bottom. Once it sinks, it stays submerged. However, once in a while, a few pebbles of poo-poo hit the water and then surface. This raises the question – why does some poo-poo float but most sink?

All poo-poo has been through the body's digestive process. Believe it or not, the majority of poo-poo is not waste from what you ate – it is dead bacteria that was on the items you ate. (It also has remnants of what you ate, bile, dead cells, water, and even cells from your intestinal lining.) Poo-poo that floats typically has got gas bubbles caught in it. That's right, it has a fart – or maybe more than one – trapped inside of it. This gas makes it buoyant. If the gas is removed, it will sink like other poo-poo.

Although a trapped fart is the reason most poo-poo floats, there are two other possibilities. It can be trapped air or fat. Floating poo-poo can also be caused by trapped air; if you eat hurriedly, you are likely swallowing a lot of air as well as food, and this air is trapped inside your body until it finds a way out. In rare cases, the floating poop is made up of fat. Normally fat gets absorbed into the body, but, once in a while, enough slips through that it causes floating poo-poo. Floating poo is nothing to worry about unless you have it every day, and then your body may need something to help it digest fats better.

Poo-poo comes in many different shapes and sizes, ranging from pellets to logs, and all of these can float as well as sink. The healthiest kind of poo-poo is a brown log or sausage that sinks, but none of the other types – sinking or floating - mean that you need to go to the doctor.

If you want to increase your odds of seeing floaters, eat beans, sugar-free candy, and high fiber foods such as broccoli. These foods stimulate the body to create gas, gas that can get caught inside poo-poo – and gas that can be embarrassing if you are riding in an elevator. One thing you can say with certainty having read this chapter – "I know my poop."

FUN FACTS

Poo-poo is brown because it contains expired red blood cells; it would be gray otherwise.

Almost 1/3 of Americans look at each and every poo-poo after wiping; doctors recommend doing this.

Abnormally stinky poo-poo is usually a sign of a stomach bug.

CONCLUSION

We live in a fascinating world!

Unfortunately, most of the time we take this world for granted. We assume that the world is the way that it is because that is the only way that it could be. However, when we start to ask "why?," we begin to understand that the world is very complex.

I hope you have enjoyed learning about the topics covered. More importantly, I hope that you have begun to appreciate asking questions and seeking answers. You are destined to be a lifelong learner; even when your official schooling is complete and there are no more teachers, no more books, and no more principals, you will need to keep asking "why?" and seek the answers to your question.

I don't know if you ever noticed, but there is the word "quest" in "question." Every question that you ask is a new adventure. I had fifty very enjoyable quests as I sought the answers to these questions. Learning is an adventure; learning is fun!

Did you enjoy the book?

If you did, we are ecstatic. If not, please write your complaint to us and we will ensure we fix it.

If you're feeling generous, there is something important that you can help me with – tell other people that you enjoyed the book.

Ask a grown-up to write about it on Amazon. When they do, more people will find out about the book. It also lets Amazon know that we are making kids around the world laugh. Even a few words and ratings would go a long way.

If you have any ideas or jokes that you think are super funny, please let us know. We would love to hear from you. Our email address is -

riddleland@riddlelandforkids.com

Other Fun Books By Riddleland Riddles Series

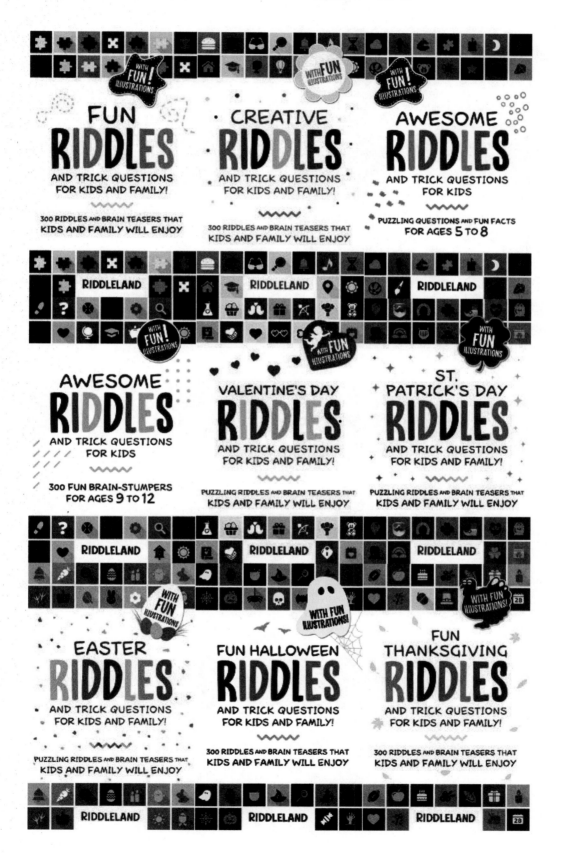

Its Laugh O'Clock Joke Books

It's Laugh O'Clock Would You Rather Books

Get them on Amazon
or our website at www.riddlelandforkids.com

About Riddleland

Riddleland is a mum + dad run publishing company. We are passionate about creating fun and innovative books to help children develop their reading skills and fall in love with reading. If you have suggestions for us or want to work with us, shoot us an email at

riddleland@riddlelandforkids.com

Our family's favorite quote:

"Creativity is an area in which younger people
have a tremendous advantage since
they have an endearing habit of always
questioning past wisdom and authority."
~ Bill Hewlett

Riddleland Bonus

Join our **Facebook Group** at
Riddleland For Kids to get daily jokes and riddles.

Bonus Book

https://pixelfy.me/riddlelandbonus

Thank you for buying this book. As a token of our appreciation, we would like to offer a special bonus—a collection of 50 original jokes, riddles, and funny stories.

REFERENCES

15 fun facts about wedding rings. Timeless Bands. (n.d.). Retrieved October 4, 2022, from https://www.timelessweddingbands.com/blog/15-Fun-Facts-About-Wedding-Rings#

5 important monogram questions answered. 5 Important Monogram Questions I Eve's Addiction. (n.d.). Retrieved October 4, 2022, from https://www.evesaddiction.com/jewelry-guide/monogram-questions-answered.html#

Adams, R. (2022, July 19). There's a lot you can do to keep neighborhood birds from flying into Windows. PawTracks. Retrieved October 5, 2022, from https://www.pawtracks.com/other-animals/why-birds-fly-into-windows/

Adams, S. (2022, May 27). What's the difference between memorial day and Veterans Day? khou.com. Retrieved October 4, 2022, from https://www.khou.com/article/news/national/military-news/memorial-day-vs-veterans-day/67-22b46299-8292-4951-ba04-0ec47222ba3e

Admin. (2014, August 29). 8 reasons you should eat dessert. Despina's cafe. Retrieved October 4, 2022, from https://www.despinascafe.com/8-reasons-you-should-eat-dessert/

Admin. (2017, May 24). Interesting facts you want to know about pillows. Mattress World. Retrieved October 5, 2022, from https://gentlehome.com/7-interesting-facts-to-know-about-pillows/

Admin. (2020, November 4). Interesting facts about desserts: Just fun facts. Just Fun Facts I Fun and interesting site. Retrieved October 4, 2022, from https://justfunfacts.com/interesting-facts-about-desserts/

Admin. (2022, August 25). Why do we have two eyes - necessity of two eyes and amblyopia. BYJUS. Retrieved October 4, 2022, from https://byjus.com/physics/why-do-we-have-two-eyes/

Admin. (2022, July 4). Interesting facts about sunsets and Sunrises. MyStart. Retrieved October 4, 2022, from https://blog.mystart.com/interesting-facts-about-sunsets-and-sunrises/

Alleah. (2022, May 23). 40 Fun Jack-o'-lantern facts for some trick or treating. Facts.net. Retrieved October 4, 2022, from https://facts.net/jack-o-lantern-facts/

Anonymous. (2005, August 15). About those flashing rear end devices... About those Flashing Rear End Devices... - Trains Magazine - Trains News Wire, Railroad News, Railroad Industry News, Web Cams, and Forms. Retrieved October 5, 2022, from https://cs.trains.com/trn/f/111/t/43141.aspx

Ansari, N. (2015, March 8). Why do we shake hands? to smell other people, scientists say. Science Times. Retrieved October 4, 2022, from https://www.sciencetimes.com/articles/3802/20150308/why-do-we-shake-hands-to-smell-other-people-scientists-say.htm

Answers Corporation. (n.d.). What year was the 3 prong outlet invented? Answers. Retrieved October 5, 2022, from https://www.answers.com/Q/What_year_was_the_3_prong_outlet_invented

Ashkenazi, S. (2017, September 17). Why do we eat dessert at the end of the meal? Retrieved October 4, 2022, from https://davidson.weizmann.ac.il/en/online/askexpert/why-do-we-eat-dessert-end-meal

Atkins, C. (2022, October 3). Why do birds poop on cars? - top 7 reasons. Thayer Birding. Retrieved October 5, 2022, from https://www.thayerbirding.com/why-do-birds-poop-on-cars/#

Author. (2012, August 30). How to make your hair grow faster. Retrieved October 5, 2022, from http://www.howtomakeyourhairgrowfast.net/know-about-different-comb-types-and-their-uses.html

Barbara. (2016, August 12). The history of monograms. The Enchanted Manor. Retrieved October 4, 2022, from https://theenchantedmanor.com/the-history-of-monograms/

Barilla, C. (2022, March 17). If you're caught not wearing green on St. Patrick's day, you might get pinched - here's why. Distractify. Retrieved October 4, 2022, from https://www.distractify.com/p/why-do-you-get-pinched-for-not-wearing-green-st-patricks-day

BBC. (2011, October 20). Religions - christianity: All hallows' eve. BBC. Retrieved October 4, 2022, from https://www.bbc.co.uk/religion/religions/christianity/holydays/halloween_1.shtml

Beans beans the magical fruit. all nursery rhymes. (n.d.). Retrieved October 5, 2022, from https://allnurseryrhymes.com/beans-beans-the-magical-fruit/

Berger, A. (n.d.). Here's why that huge cotton ball comes in pill bottles. Business Insider. Retrieved October 5, 2022, from https://www.businessinsider.com/why-huge-cotton-ball-comes-pill-bottles-medicine-health-pharmacy-prescription-2017-5

Birdvet. (2021, October 25). Why do birds fly into windows? AvianVets.org. Retrieved October 5, 2022, from https://avianvets.org/why-do-birds-fly-into-windows/

Bliss, M. (2015, September 6). SIOWFA15: Science in our world: Certainty and controversy. SiOWfa15 Science in Our World Certainty and Controversy. Retrieved October 4, 2022, from https://sites.psu.edu/siowfa15/2015/09/06/why-do-we-shake-hands/

Bogard, M. O. (n.d.). History of the prescription bottle. American Institute of the History of Pharmacy. Retrieved October 5, 2022, from https://aihp.org/slide_talk/history-of-the-prescription-bottle/

Borel, B. (2022, March 18). Why do bulls charge when they see red? LiveScience. Retrieved October 4, 2022, from https://www.livescience.com/33700-bulls-charge-red.html

Brunner, B. (2021, December 10). A history of the New Year. Infoplease. Retrieved October 4, 2022, from https://www.infoplease.com/culture-entertainment/holidays/history-new-year

Burgess, T. (n.d.). Why Do We Celebrate Birthdays with Cake? EHow. Retrieved October 4, 2022, from https://www.ehow.com/about_6610582_do-celebrate-birthdays-cake_.html

Button. Ten Random Facts. (2016, March 15). Retrieved October 5, 2022, from https://tenrandomfacts.com/button/

Byron, J., Stitzer, C., & Spinner, M. A. (n.d.). Christmas tree facts. Christmas Tree Facts - Christmas Trees and More - University of Illinois Extension. Retrieved October 4, 2022, from https://web.extension.illinois.edu/trees/facts.cfm#

Carroll, D. (2021, June 6). Your guide to what Social Security Numbers mean. Social Security Intelligence. Retrieved October 4, 2022, from https://www.socialsecurityintelligence.com/what-social-security-numbers-mean/#

CC Sunscreens. (2017, January 13). 15 interesting facts you didn't know about windows. CC Sunscreen. Retrieved October 5, 2022, from https://ccsunscreens.com/15-interesting-facts-about-windows/

Cindy. (2022, March 8). Why are men and women's shirt buttons on opposite sides? Bud's Dry Cleaning. Retrieved October 5, 2022, from https://budsdrycleaning.com/why-are-men-and-womens-shirt-buttons-on-opposite-sides/#

CMR Products. (2015, December 9). Truck hitch – end of train device. CMR Products. Retrieved October 5, 2022, from https://www.cmrproducts.com/truck-hitch-end-of-train-device/

Comb. Ten Random Facts. (2014, August 10). Retrieved October 5, 2022, from https://tenrandomfacts.com/comb/

Comeau, J. B. (2020, January 1). New Year toasting: Origins, dos and don'ts - étiquette Julie. Etiquette Julie Blais Comeau. Retrieved October 4, 2022, from https://etiquettejulie.com/new-year-toasting-origins-and-donts/#

Conley, J. (2022, January 8). Why pinch on saint patrick day. St Margarets school. Retrieved October 4, 2022, from https://www.stmargschool.com/blog/why-pinch-on-saint-patrick-day.html

Cotton. The story of cotton- history of Cotton. (n.d.). Retrieved October 5, 2022, from https://www.cotton.org/pubs/cottoncounts/story/

Cross, L. (2019, November 29). The reason buttons on men's and women's shirts are on different sides - the list. TheList.com. Retrieved October 5, 2022, from https://www.thelist.com/177015/the-reason-buttons-on-mens-and-womens-shirts-are-on-different-sides/

Curious kids: Why do people in different countries speak different languages? The Conversation. (2020, February 6). Retrieved October 4, 2022, from https://theconversation.com/curious-kids-why-do-people-in-different-countries-speak-different-languages-127112

The Daily Meal Staff. (2018, July 11). 12 things you didn't know about Fortune cookies gallery. TheDailyMeal.com. Retrieved October 4, 2022, from https://www.thedailymeal.com/eat/fortune-cookie-facts-gallery/slide-9

David, E. (2020, December 28). The true history of the horseshoe - grunge. Grunge. com. Retrieved October 5, 2022, from https://www.grunge.com/303114/the-true-history-of-the-horseshoe/

Davies, C. (n.d.). Why pillows turn yellow - and how to tell if they're healthy to sleep on. MSN. Retrieved October 5, 2022, from https://www.msn.com/en-us/lifestyle/shopping/why-pillows-turn-yellow-and-how-to-tell-if-they-re-healthy-to-sleep-on/ar-AATivp1

Denby, L. (2021, December 22). Why do we carve pumpkins for Halloween? the real reason might just surprise you. Taste of Home. Retrieved October 4, 2022, from https://www.tasteofhome.com/article/history-lesson-why-do-we-carve-pumpkins/

Digitsite. (2014, April 23). Why are the keyboard keys arranged as QWERTYUIOPASDFGHJKLZXCVBNM? digitsite's Blog. Retrieved October 5, 2022, from https://digitsite.wordpress.com/2014/04/23/why-is-the-keyboard-keys-arranged-as-qwertyuiopasdfghjklzxcvbnm/#

Edgar (aka MrConsumer). (2013, August 5). The Little Secret Inside that Big Pill Bottle. Mouse Print*. Retrieved October 5, 2022, from https://www.mouseprint.org/2013/08/05/the-little-secret-inside-that-big-pill-bottle/

Editorial Staff. (2022, July 25). 45 interesting facts about computers. The Fact File. Retrieved October 5, 2022, from https://thefactfile.org/computer-facts/

Editorial Staff. (2022, July 25). 45 interesting facts about computers. The Fact File. Retrieved October 5, 2022, from https://thefactfile.org/computer-facts/

Edwards, B. T. (2022, May 14). Symbolism of lady justice. The Classroom | Empowering Students in Their College Journey. Retrieved October 4, 2022, from https://www.theclassroom.com/symbolism-of-lady-justice-12080961.html

Encyclopædia Britannica, inc. (n.d.). Cupid. Encyclopædia Britannica. Retrieved October 4, 2022, from https://www.britannica.com/topic/Cupid

Encyclopædia Britannica, inc. (n.d.). Why do we carve pumpkins at Halloween? Encyclopædia Britannica. Retrieved October 4, 2022, from https://www.britannica.com/story/why-do-we-carve-pumpkins-at-halloween

The evolution of the military salute. EnglishClub. (n.d.). Retrieved October 4, 2022, from https://www.englishclub.com/efl/podcasts/interesting-facts/salute/#

Fact or fiction: Licking a wound helps it heal faster. New England Baptist Hospital. (2018, September 25). Retrieved October 5, 2022, from https://www.nebh.org/blog/fact-or-fiction-licking-a-wound-helps-it-heal-faster/

FAQ: Roman IIII vs. IV on clock dials. Electric Time Company. (2016, October 7). Retrieved October 4, 2022, from https://www.electrictime.com/news/roman-iiii-vs-iv-on-clock-dials/#

Ferro, S. (2015, June 16). Why are public toilet seats U-shaped? Mental Floss. Retrieved October 5, 2022, from https://www.mentalfloss.com/article/64677/why-are-public-toilet-seats-u-shaped

Ferro, S. (2017, June 21). Why do people in the UK drive on the left side of the road? Mental Floss. Retrieved October 5, 2022, from https://www.mentalfloss.com/article/501958/why-do-people-uk-drive-left-side-road#

Finkel, R. (2012, October 21). Why is there cotton in my medicine bottle? Drugsdb.com. Retrieved October 5, 2022, from https://www.drugsdb.com/blog/why-is-there-cotton-in-my-medicine-bottle.html#

Finney, L. (2016, July 14). Here's the odd reason why women's shirts button on the left. TODAY.com. Retrieved October 5, 2022, from https://www.today.com/style/here-s-why-men-s-women-s-shirts-button-opposite-t100380

Flashing rear end device (FRED). Brick Train Depot. (n.d.). Retrieved October 5, 2022, from https://bricktraindepot.com/shop/accessories/flashing-rear-end-device-fred/

Flashing rear-end device. Flashing Rear-end Device | Technology Trends. (n.d.). Retrieved October 5, 2022, from https://www.primidi.com/flashing_rear_end_device

Fontinelle, A. (2022, July 13). The purpose of having a Social Security number. Investopedia. Retrieved October 4, 2022, from https://www.investopedia.com/articles/personal-finance/050615/purpose-having-social-security-number.asp#

Fred (flashing rear end device). Trainorders.com Discussion. (n.d.). Retrieved October 5, 2022, from https://www.trainorders.com/discussion/read.php?1%2C3547353
Funny World Birthday Trivia. Funny world birthday trivia. (n.d.). Retrieved October 4, 2022, from https://www.nobleworkscards.com/birthday-world-trivia.html

Gavin, M. (2017, July 17). Why do human beings speak so many languages? Scientific American. Retrieved October 4, 2022, from https://www.scientificamerican.com/article/why-do-human-beings-speak-so-many-languages/

George, R. (2020, January 2). A brief history of plumbing codes " Working pressure. Working Pressure. Retrieved October 5, 2022, from https://www.workingpressuremag.com/a-brief-history-of-plumbing-codes/#

Gillespie, C. (2022, May 27). Why Americans and Brits drive on different sides of the road. Reader's Digest. Retrieved October 5, 2022, from https://www.rd.com/article/why-drive-on-different-sides-of-the-road/

Gravedigger. (2016, February 12). Front door superstitions. Burial Day Books. Retrieved October 5, 2022, from https://burialday.com/front-door-superstitions/

Guardian News and Media. (n.d.). RED TAPE, WHITE LIES. The Guardian. Retrieved October 4, 2022, from https://www.theguardian.com/notesandqueries/query/0,5753,-1487,00.html

Guberman, J. (2016, August 2). Why is poo number 2? The Odyssey Online. Retrieved October 5, 2022, from https://www.theodysseyonline.com/pee-number-1-poo-number-2

Half-full pill bottles for sale - consumer reports. Half-Full Pill Bottles for Sale - Consumer Reports. (2013, August 1). Retrieved October 5, 2022, from https://www.consumerreports.org/cro/magazine/2013/08/pill-bottles-with-air-to-spare/index.htm

Haney, E. M. (2019, October 17). Why do we shake hands? The Odyssey Online. Retrieved October 4, 2022, from https://www.theodysseyonline.com/why-shake-hands

The Healthline Editorial Team. (2017, December 19). American gut check: How our nation poops. Healthline. Retrieved October 5, 2022, from https://www.healthline.com/health/american-gut-check

Healthline Media. (n.d.). Why do my farts smell so bad? causes and prevention methods. Healthline. Retrieved October 5, 2022, from https://www.healthline.com/health/smelly-farts#complications

Heichelbech, R. (2021, December 20). Why do people say "hello" when answering the phone? Dusty Old Thing. Retrieved October 4, 2022, from https://dustyoldthing.com/hello-answer-the-phone/

Heichelbech, R. (2021, March 12). The reason why horseshoes are considered lucky. Dusty Old Thing. Retrieved October 5, 2022, from https://dustyoldthing.com/lucky-horseshoe-history/#

Helmenstine, A. M. (2019, March 25). Why do we yawn? A look at the reasons. ThoughtCo. Retrieved October 5, 2022, from https://www.thoughtco.com/why-do-we-yawn-4586495

Heshmat , S. (2015, April 23). What is confirmation bias? Psychology Today. Retrieved October 4, 2022, from https://www.psychologytoday.com/us/blog/science-choice/201504/what-is-confirmation-bias

The history of earth day. Earth Day. (2022, May 11). Retrieved October 4, 2022, from https://www.earthday.org/history/

History of Groundhog Day. VisitPA. (2022, July 1). Retrieved October 4, 2022, from https://www.visitpa.com/story-idea/history-groundhog-day#

The history of the Stoplight. Mast Service Center Inc. (2021, June 6). Retrieved October 5, 2022, from https://mastservicecenter.net/the-history-of-the-stoplight/

History.com Editors. (2009, December 22). History of valentine's day. History.com. Retrieved October 4, 2022, from https://www.history.com/topics/valentines-day/history-of-valentines-day-2

History.com Editors. (2009, October 27). History of christmas trees. History.com. Retrieved October 4, 2022, from https://www.history.com/topics/christmas/history-of-christmas-trees

History.com Editors. (2010, February 16). New Year's. History.com. Retrieved October 4, 2022, from https://www.history.com/topics/holidays/new-years

Hocken, V. (n.d.). The 12 months of the Year. 12 Months of the Year. Retrieved October 4, 2022, from https://www.timeanddate.com/calendar/months/

Holland, J. (2022, January 19). Why do bulls hate red? Johnny Holland. Johnny Holland. Retrieved October 4, 2022, from https://johnnyholland.org/2022/01/why-do-bulls-hate-red/#r

Hoyt, A. (2020, August 20). 10 ways animals supposedly predict the weather. HowStuffWorks Science. Retrieved October 4, 2022, from https://science.howstuffworks.com/nature/climate-weather/storms/10-ways-animals-supposedly-predict-the-weather.htm#

Hrustic, A., Matthews, M., & Benton, E. (2021, November 29). These 15 foods are the reason you're always farting. Men's Health. Retrieved October 5, 2022, from https://www.menshealth.com/health/a19546650/foods-that-make-you-fart/

Huddleston, J. (2019, December 4). The real reason donuts have holes - mashed. Mashed.com. Retrieved October 4, 2022, from https://www.mashed.com/177570/the-real-reason-donuts-have-holes/

Humaira. (2022, April 24). Why do birds poop on cars? (2 possible reasons). Birdcageshere. Retrieved October 5, 2022, from https://birdcageshere.com/2022/04/24/why-do-birds-poop-on-cars/

Hunt, C. (2022, June 9). How to put out a campfire - FFG. Firefighter Garage. Retrieved October 5, 2022, from https://firefightergarage.com/how-to-put-out-a-campfire/#

James, R. (2021, January 20). 41 electric facts about electricity: Fact City. Facts. Retrieved October 5, 2022, from https://factcity.com/facts-about-electricity/#

James. (2016, September 27). Christmas tree facts. Primary Facts. Retrieved October 4, 2022, from https://primaryfacts.com/2840/christmas-tree-facts/#

Jamieson, M. (2022, August 30). The real meaning behind the lady of justice statues. Heather & Little. Retrieved October 4, 2022, from https://heatherandlittle.com/blog/restoration/the-meaning-behind-the-lady-of-justice-statue/

Jason. (2017, September 24). 25 booger facts you probably didn't know. List25. Retrieved October 5, 2022, from https://list25.com/25-booger-facts-you-probably-didnt-know/

Jenna, J. (2021, May 31). What's up weather with Jordyn: Can dogs predict the weather? WNCT. Retrieved October 4, 2022, from https://www.wnct.com/weather/whats-up-weather-with-jordyn-can-dogs-predict-the-weather/#

Johnson, C. (2022, September 26). Why throwing rice at weddings is totally okay. theknot.com. Retrieved October 4, 2022, from https://www.theknot.com/content/youre-allowed-to-throw-rice-at-weddings

Kagan, M. (n.d.). Why are boogers salty? Whyzz tools for worldwise family conversations. Retrieved October 5, 2022, from https://www.whyzz.com/stories/why-are-boogers-salty

Kandpal, D. (2022, February 1). Meaning of groundhog sees his shadow explained ahead of 2022 festival. HITC. Retrieved October 4, 2022, from https://www.hitc.com/en-gb/2022/02/01/groundhog-sees-shadow-meaning/

Katie. (2020, November 18). Why do we speak different languages? Language Trainers USA Blog. Retrieved October 4, 2022, from https://www.languagetrainers.com/blog/why-different-languages/

Kendle, K. (2020, June 4). Teach your kids how to say hello in 25 languages. Travel with Monsters. Retrieved October 4, 2022, from https://travelwithmonsters.com/2018/12/teach-your-kids-how-to-say-hello-in-25-languages/

Kerley, D. A. (2014, January 2). Why do we blow out candles on birthday cakes? Mental Floss. Retrieved October 4, 2022, from https://www.mentalfloss.com/article/54069/why-do-we-blow-out-candles-birthday-cakes

Khawaja, A. A. (2022, January 24). 4 reasons why do horses need shoes. Keeping Pet. Retrieved October 5, 2022, from https://keepingpet.com/why-do-horses-need-shoes/#

Khrais, R. (2012, December 31). Why we toast: Uncorking A New Year's tradition. NPR. Retrieved October 4, 2022, from https://www.npr.org/sections/thesalt/2012/12/31/166576144/why-we-toast-uncorking-a-new-years-tradition

Kidadl Team. (2022, September 8). Why do donuts have holes sweet treats explained for kids. Kidadl. Retrieved October 4, 2022, from https://kidadl.com/fun-facts/why-do-donuts-have-holes-sweet-treats-explained-for-kids

Kids math. Ducksters. (n.d.). Retrieved October 4, 2022, from https://www.ducksters.com/kidsmath/roman_numerals.php#

Kidsplayandcreate. (2015, September 24). Funny things about poop for kids. Kids Play and Create. Retrieved October 5, 2022, from https://www.kidsplayandcreate.com/funny-things-about-poop-for-kids/#

Lady justice facts for kids. Lady Justice Facts for Kids. (n.d.). Retrieved October 4, 2022, from https://kids.kiddle.co/Lady_Justice#

Laliberte, M. (2022, June 13). This is why we wear wedding rings on the fourth finger. Reader's Digest. Retrieved October 4, 2022, from https://www.rd.com/article/wedding-rings-ring-finger/

Lehnardt, K. (2016, November 22). 48 interesting facts about kissing. Interesting Facts. Retrieved October 5, 2022, from https://www.factretriever.com/kissing-facts

Lehnardt, K. (2016, September 25). 100 interesting facts about urine. Interesting Facts. Retrieved October 5, 2022, from https://www.factretriever.com/urine-facts

Lewis, D. (2021, April 20). What are the origins of saluting? . 60 Sec Fun Facts. Retrieved October 4, 2022, from https://60secfunfacts.com/history/why-do-we-salut/

Light yellow urine color. Light Yellow Urine. (n.d.). Retrieved October 5, 2022, from https://www.urinecolors.com/urine-color/light-yellow-urine/

Lingoda Team. (2022, May 31). Discover 30 fun facts about the English language. Lingoda. Retrieved October 4, 2022, from https://blog.lingoda.com/en/fun-facts-english-language/#

Link, R. (2021, March 18). Why do beans make you fart? Healthline. Retrieved October 5, 2022, from https://www.healthline.com/nutrition/why-do-beans-make-you-fart

Long history of combs and brush. SkyFox. (2021, December 18). Retrieved October 5, 2022, from https://skyfoxtv.com/long-history-of-combs-and-brush/

Lubin, G. (n.d.). The scientific reasons why we eat dessert last. Business Insider. Retrieved October 4, 2022, from https://www.businessinsider.com/why-we-eat-dessert-last-2016-11

Lyons, C. (2014, October 27). Why you should never pee on the fire. Backpacker. Retrieved October 5, 2022, from https://www.backpacker.com/survival/why-you-should-never-pee-on-the-fire/

Magazine Monitor. (2015, January 5). Who, what, why: Why does the military insist on saluting? BBC News. Retrieved October 4, 2022, from https://www.bbc.com/news/blogs-magazine-monitor-30679406

Mahbub. (2019, February 28). Fun facts about toilets: EAGO parts.com (recommended). EAGO Parts.Com. Retrieved October 5, 2022, from https://eagoparts.com/fun-facts-about-toilets/?doing_wp_cron=1652822842.8483080863952636718750#.YoQTPozMKUk

Mammadli, R. (2019, February 10). Causes of thick rubbery mucus from nose. Health Recovery Tips. Retrieved October 5, 2022, from https://iytmed.com/causes-of-thick-rubbery-mucus-from-nose/

Masters, K. (2015, June 27). Why is a day divided into 24 hours? (intermediate). Home - Curious About Astronomy? Ask an Astronomer. Retrieved October 4, 2022, from http://curious.astro.cornell.edu/our-solar-system/161-our-solar-system/the-earth/day-night-cycle/761-why-is-a-day-divided-into-24-hours-intermediate

Mattern, J. L. (2020, September 20). 15 things you didn't know you could monogram. Country Living. Retrieved October 4, 2022, from https://www.countryliving.com/shopping/g4240/things-you-didnt-know-you-could-monogram/#

Matthew R. (2022, September 14). Why are pencils yellow? Toyz School. Retrieved October 5, 2022, from https://toyzschool.com/why-are-pencils-yellow/

McFadden, C. (2020, June 12). The origin of the term 'computer bug'. Interesting Engineering. Retrieved October 5, 2022, from https://interestingengineering.com/the-origin-of-the-term-computer-bug

MediLexicon International. (2018, April 11). How often should you pee? what's normal and what's perfect? Medical News Today. Retrieved October 5, 2022, from https://www.medicalnewstoday.com/articles/321461

Mehdi, R. (2022, May 31). Origin story: Why do we say hello when answering the phone? BYJUS Blog. Retrieved October 4, 2022, from https://blog.byjus.com/knowledge-vine/origin-story-why-do-we-say-hello-when-answering-the-phone/

Merriam-Webster. (n.d.). Origin and spelling of Halloween (or Hallowe'en). Merriam-Webster. Retrieved October 4, 2022, from https://www.merriam-webster.com/words-at-play/halloween-origin-spelling

Midnightpanther. (n.d.). Why doorknobs are far away from the hinges. APlusPhysics Community. Retrieved October 5, 2022, from https://aplusphysics.com/community/index.php?%2Fblogs%2Fentry%2F737-why-doorknobs-are-far-away-from-the-hinges%2F

Miklovic, S. (2022, February 2). Will the groundhog see his shadow today? TheNBXpress.com. Retrieved October 4, 2022, from https://www.thenbxpress.com/will-the-groundhog-see-his-shadow-today/

Mills, A. (2018, September 2). Why do bulls attack the color red? animalwised.com. Retrieved October 4, 2022, from https://www.animalwised.com/why-do-bulls-attack-the-color-red-2802.html#

The Monogram Company. (2019, October 24). 5 interesting embroidery facts - the monogram company. connect2local. Retrieved October 4, 2022, from https://connect2local.com/l/147556/c/748608/5-interesting-embroidery-facts

Moss, D. (2017, November 23). Outdoor Education: Fun campfire facts. PE Update.com - Physical Education Lesson Plans, Activities, Games, Tips. Retrieved October 5, 2022, from https://www.physicaleducationupdate.com/public/373.cfm#

Nadim, K. (2022, April 22). Why do birds keep pooping on my car? Birds Advice. Birds Advice. Retrieved October 5, 2022, from https://www.birdsadvice.com/why-do-birds-keep-pooping-on-my-car/

Nall, R. (2018, July 19). Clear urine: Causes, frequent, pregnancy, diabetes, uti, and more. Healthline. Retrieved October 5, 2022, from https://www.healthline.com/health/clear-urine#causes

NASA. (n.d.). Why does the sun rise in the east and set in the West? NASA. Retrieved October 4, 2022, from https://starchild.gsfc.nasa.gov/docs/StarChild/questions/question14.html

Nature curiosity: Why do birds fly into windows? Accelerator. (2021, February 17). Retrieved October 5, 2022, from https://www.reconnectwithnature.org/News-Events/The-Buzz/Nature-Curiosity-Why-Do-Birds-Fly-Into-Windows

Nieboer, G. (n.d.). A.K.A. Button Button Who's Got the Button? Hide the button. Retrieved October 5, 2022, from http://www.gameskidsplay.net/games/sensing_games/hide_the_button.htm

On determining the proper question by Albert Einstein - Gurteen. (n.d.). Retrieved October 4, 2022, from http://www.gurteen.com/gurteen/gurteen.nsf/id/determining-the-proper-question

O'Shaughnessy, L. (2010, July 22). Why are pencils yellow? CBS News. Retrieved October 5, 2022, from https://www.cbsnews.com/news/why-are-pencils-yellow/

Pagán, A. (2021, March 12). Candles, wishes, and the history behind our birthday cake traditions. The Takeout. Retrieved October 4, 2022, from https://thetakeout.com/why-do-we-eat-birthday-cake-and-blow-out-candles-1846445957

Pask, S. (2021, February 8). A guide to rings for men: What rings mean on each finger. The Modest Man. Retrieved October 4, 2022, from https://www.themodestman.com/rings-for-men/#

Patterson, S. (2020, October 13). Why was Rice Thrown at a wedding? Courageous Christian Father. Retrieved October 4, 2022, from https://www.courageouschristianfather.com/why-was-rice-thrown-at-a-wedding/

Pediatrics. (2019, October 22). What boogers say about your health. Scripps Health. Retrieved October 5, 2022, from https://www.scripps.org/news_items/6831-5-fun-facts-about-boogers

Penzo, L. (2020, February 11). 18 fast facts you didn't know about Social Security numbers. Len Penzo dot Com. Retrieved October 4, 2022, from https://lenpenzo.com/blog/id1510-18-fast-facts-you-didnt-know-about-social-security-numbers-2.html

Perkins, C. (2020, July 28). The bizarre reason some countries drive on the left. Road & Track. Retrieved October 5, 2022, from https://www.roadandtrack.com/car-culture/a19980496/why-uk-drives-on-left/

Powell, H. (2022, August 30). Why birds hit windows-and how you can help prevent it. All About Birds. Retrieved October 5, 2022, from https://www.allaboutbirds.org/news/why-birds-hit-windows-and-how-you-can-help-prevent-it/

Powers, R. (2019, June 25). Origins and use of the U.S. military hand salute. LiveAbout. Retrieved October 4, 2022, from https://www.thebalancecareers.com/u-s-military-salute-3331994

Prajapati, M. (2019, May 13). Why is dessert eaten at the end of the meal? timesknowledge.in. Retrieved October 4, 2022, from https://www.timesknowledge.in/history/why-is-dessert-eaten-at-the-end-of-the-meal-1872-3.html

Preidt, R. (2018, May 25). Are yawns really contagious? WebMD. Retrieved October 5, 2022, from https://www.webmd.com/brain/news/20180525/are-yawns-really-contagious

Prithyani, K. (2019, September 16). If Red Means Emergency, why are exit signs green? Medium. Retrieved October 5, 2022, from https://uxdesign.cc/if-red-means-emergency-why-are-exit-signs-green-111760c217c1

Prudentia - the roman goddess of discipline (Roman mythology). Godchecker. (n.d.). Retrieved October 4, 2022, from https://www.godchecker.com/roman-mythology/PRUDENTIA/

Pruitt, S. (2017, May 25). The WWI origins of the poppy as a remembrance symbol. History.com. Retrieved October 4, 2022, from https://www.history.com/news/world-war-i-poppy-remembrance-symbol-veterans-day

Puiu, T. (2016, September 16). Is licking your wounds actually a good thing? ZME Science. Retrieved October 5, 2022, from https://www.zmescience.com/science/licking-wounds-good-or-bad/

Purdie, J. (2020, February 5). Why do we yawn and is it contagious? Healthline. Retrieved October 5, 2022, from https://www.healthline.com/health/why-do-we-yawn#takeaway

Quora .com. (2018, January 29). Why are the keys on a QWERTY keyboard laid out as they are? Mental Floss. Retrieved October 5, 2022, from https://www.mentalfloss.com/article/527266/why-are-keys-qwerty-keyboard-laid-out-they-are

Radford, B. (2010, July 6). Why are men's and women's buttons on opposite sides? LiveScience. Retrieved October 5, 2022, from https://www.livescience.com/32681-why-are-mens-and-womens-buttons-on-opposite-sides.html

Rehberger, G. (n.d.). The month of February. February: Second Month of the Year. Retrieved October 4, 2022, from https://www.timeanddate.com/calendar/months/february.html

Rehberger, G. (n.d.). The month of January. January: First Month of the Year. Retrieved October 4, 2022, from https://www.timeanddate.com/calendar/months/january.html

Rehberger, G. (n.d.). The month of June. timeanddate.com. Retrieved October 4, 2022, from https://www.timeanddate.com/calendar/months/june.html

Rehberger, G. (n.d.). The month of March. March: Third Month of the Year. Retrieved October 4, 2022, from https://www.timeanddate.com/calendar/months/march.html

Rehberger, G. (n.d.). The month of May. May: Fifth Month of the Year. Retrieved October 4, 2022, from https://www.timeanddate.com/calendar/months/may.html

Rev. Saunders, W. (n.d.). History of st. valentine. Catholic Education Resource Center. Retrieved October 4, 2022, from https://www.catholiceducation.org/en/culture/catholic-contributions/history-of-st-valentine.html

Rhys, D. (2020, August 31). Lady justice – symbolism and meaning. Symbol Sage. Retrieved October 4, 2022, from https://symbolsage.com/lady-justice-meaning/

Rocheleau, J. (2014, June 27). Where does the sun go at night? why does it disappear? Planet Facts. Retrieved October 4, 2022, from https://planetfacts.org/where-does-the-sun-go-at-night/#

Sager, J. (2022, April 22). 50 Earth Day trivia questions and answers to inspire you to protect the planet - parade: Entertainment, recipes, health, life, holidays. Parade. Retrieved October 4, 2022, from https://parade.com/1192402/jessicasager/earth-day-trivia/

Saini, A. (2020, March 11). Why is an hour 60 minutes long? let's find out. RapidLeaksIndia. Retrieved October 4, 2022, from https://rapidleaks.com/science/why-is-an-hour-60-minutes-long/

Sanchez, M. (2022, August 16). What your poop says about your health. HealthPartners Blog. Retrieved October 5, 2022, from https://www.healthpartners.com/blog/healthy-poop-chart/

Sbszipper. (2018, May 28). A brief history of buttons through the ages. Decorative Zips and Fashion Trend. Retrieved October 5, 2022, from https://www.sbs-zipper.com/blog/a-brief-history-of-buttons-through-the-ages/

Scientific American. (2007, March 5). Why is a minute divided into 60 seconds, an hour into 60 minutes, yet there are only 24 hours in a day? Scientific American. Retrieved October 4, 2022, from https://www.scientificamerican.com/article/experts-time-division-days-hours-minutes/

Sep 9, 1947 CE: World's first computer bug. National Geographic Society. (n.d.). Retrieved October 5, 2022, from https://www.nationalgeographic.org/thisday/sep9/worlds-first-computer-bug/

Shobhit. (2017, May 7). Why is a software bug called a bug? Pilanites. Retrieved October 5, 2022, from https://www.pilanites.com/software-bug-origin/#

Singh, R. (2020, July 8). Why do we have two eyes for vision and not just one. PaidForArticles. Retrieved October 4, 2022, from https://paidforarticles.com/why-do-we-have-two-eyes-for-vision-and-not-just-one-40494

Smee, T. (2019, October 8). Why do people use the word "hello" when answering the phone? thevintagenews. Retrieved October 4, 2022, from https://www.thevintagenews.com/2018/08/16/why-do-people-say-hello/?edg-c=1

Smith, D. (2022, September 4). Why do pillows turn yellow? - down & Feather Co.. Green and black abstract painting for Down & Feather. Retrieved October 5, 2022, from https://www.downandfeathercompany.com/blogs/news/the-dirty-secrets-of-your-pillows-why-your-pillows-turn-yellow

Smith, K. (2021, July 27). 12 Wound Care Fun Facts. WCEI. Retrieved October 5, 2022, from https://blog.wcei.net/12-wound-care-fun-facts

Smithsonian Magazine. (2015, November 23). Here's why men's and women's clothes button on opposite sides. Smithsonian.com. Retrieved October 5, 2022, from https://www.smithsonianmag.com/smart-news/heres-why-mens-and-womens-clothes-button-opposite-sides-1-180957361/

Soniak, M. (2012, June 14). Why are traffic lights red and green? Mental Floss. Retrieved October 5, 2022, from https://www.mentalfloss.com/article/30921/why-are-traffic-lights-red-and-green

Soniak, M. (2012, May 23). Why do beans make you fart? Mental Floss. Retrieved October 5, 2022, from https://www.mentalfloss.com/article/30748/why-do-beans-make-you-fart

Sporcle. (2018, September 20). Why are stoplights red, yellow, and green?: Sporcle blog. The Sporcle Blog. Retrieved October 5, 2022, from https://www.sporcle.com/blog/2018/09/why-are-stoplights-red-yellow-and-green/

Spotlight on...old English collection door handles. Suffolk Latch Company. (n.d.). Retrieved October 5, 2022, from https://www.suffolklatchcompany.com/blogs/news/a-brief-history-of-the-door-handle

Stacey, J. D. (2021, November 5). Science says Kissing Your Child's 'boo-boos' actually works. Medium. Retrieved October 5, 2022, from https://medium.com/modern-parent/science-says-kissing-your-childs-boo-boos-actually-works-7836d4c58982

Staff Writer. (2020, March 25). Why are typewriter keys arranged the way they are? Reference. Retrieved October 5, 2022, from https://www.reference.com/world-view/typewriter-keys-arranged-way-d84a905006a719ec

Steelman, L. (2018, March 16). Why do you get pinched on St. Patrick's day? Real Simple. Retrieved October 4, 2022, from https://www.realsimple.com/holidays-entertaining/st-patricks-day-pinch-rules#

Story of the jack O' lantern & pumpkins- history I mocomi kids. mocomi. (n.d.). Retrieved October 4, 2022, from https://mocomi.com/why-do-we-carve-pumpkins-on-halloween/

StrangeAgo. (2017, July 26). 10 weird superstitions about doors. Strange Ago. Retrieved October 5, 2022, from https://strangeago.com/2017/07/27/10-weird-superstitions-doors/

Streit, L. (2022, May 4). The 9 healthiest beans and legumes you can eat. Healthline. Retrieved October 5, 2022, from https://www.healthline.com/nutrition/healthiest-beans-legumes

Stromberg, J. (2015, January 22). Everybody poops. but here are 9 surprising facts about feces you may not know. Vox. Retrieved October 5, 2022, from https://www.vox.com/2015/1/22/7871579/poop-feces

Take online courses. earn college credit. Research Schools, Degrees & Careers. Study.com I Take Online Courses. Earn College Credit. Research Schools, Degrees & Careers. (n.d.). Retrieved October 4, 2022, from https://study.com/academy/lesson/st-valentine-lesson-for-kids-facts-biography.html

Taylor, M. (2021, April 15). Why do beans make you fart? causes, how to control gas. Greatist. Retrieved October 5, 2022, from https://greatist.com/health/why-do-beans-make-you-fart

Team SafeSleep. (2022, February 8). Why do pillows turn yellow? □. Safe Sleep Systems. Retrieved October 5, 2022, from https://safesleepsystems.com/why-do-pillows-turn-yellow/

This is the fascinating reason why doughnuts have holes. Retro Bunny. (2020, April 5). Retrieved October 4, 2022, from https://www.retrobunny.org/this-is-the-fascinating-reason-why-doughnuts-have-holes/

TimKyleElectric. (2020, December 23). The difference between two- and three-prong outlets. Tim Kyle Electric. Retrieved October 5, 2022, from https://timkyleelectric.com/outlets/the-difference-between-two-and-three-prong-outlets/

Todd. (2020, March 2). Celebrating the caboose: Five facts you didn't know. Southeastern Railway Museum. Retrieved October 5, 2022, from https://www.train-museum.org/2018/03/05/celebrating-the-caboose-five-facts-you-didnt-know/

Top 10 random but interesting facts about doors. US Window & Door. (n.d.). Retrieved October 5, 2022, from https://www.uswindow-door.com/blog/top-10-random-but-interesting-facts-about-doors

True or false: Licking a wound can promote healing. Winchester Hospital. (n.d.). Retrieved October 5, 2022, from https://www.winchesterhospital.org/health-library/article?id=157011

ULTIMATE GUIDE TO BUILDING A CAMPFIRE I HOW TO BUILD A CAMPFIRE. Koa. com. (n.d.). Retrieved October 5, 2022, from https://koa.com/blog/how-to-build-the-perfect-campfire/#

umar.bajwa1988. (2021, September 18). Old Customs or deeper meanings why do they throw rice at weddings? Old Customs or Deeper Meanings Why Do They Throw Rice at Weddings? Retrieved October 4, 2022, from https://racinepost.com/old-customs-or-deeper-meanings-why-do-they-throw-rice-at-weddings/

The unspoken reasons why we shake hands. Big Think. (2021, September 30). Retrieved October 4, 2022, from https://bigthink.com/wikimind/the-unspoken-reasons-why-we-shake-hands/

The US Sun. (2021, September 28). Why are there Interstate Highways in Hawaii? The US Sun. Retrieved October 5, 2022, from https://www.the-sun.com/news/3280805/interstate-highways-hawaii-road-system/#

VanSchmus, E. (2021, November 23). 22 inspiring New Year's toasts to ring in the New Year. Better Homes & Gardens. Retrieved October 4, 2022, from https://www.bhg.com/holidays/new-years/crafts/new-years-toasts/#

Vedantu. (2022, April 27). Why do we have two eyes? VEDANTU. Retrieved October 4, 2022, from https://www.vedantu.com/physics/why-do-we-have-two-eyes

Vogadori, A. (2021, December 22). New Year's eve toast: History, curiosities and bubbles to celebrate. Amarone della Valpolicella Vogadori. Retrieved October 4, 2022, from https://www.vogadorivini.it/en/new-years-eve-toast-history-curiosities-and-bubbles-to-celebrate/

Watson, K. (2022, January 27). Urine Color chart: What's normal and when to see a doctor. Healthline. Retrieved October 5, 2022, from https://www.healthline.com/health/urine-color-chart

Webb, P. (2022, October 3). Why are public toilet seats U-shaped - detailed answer. Save Our Water Rebates. Retrieved October 5, 2022, from https://www.saveourwaterrebates.com/why-are-public-toilet-seats-u-shaped/#

WebMD Editorial Contributors. (2021, May 26). Why do stools float sometimes? WebMD. Retrieved October 5, 2022, from https://www.webmd.com/digestive-disorders/what-to-know-about-floating-stools

What is the history behind number 'one' being a sign for pee ... - quora. Quora. (n.d.). Retrieved October 5, 2022, from https://www.quora.com/What-is-the-history-behind-number-one-being-a-sign-for-pee-and-number-two-for-poo

Who is Punxsutawney Phil? Wonderopolis. (n.d.). Retrieved October 4, 2022, from https://www.wonderopolis.org/wonder/who-is-punxsutawney-phil

Why 12 months in a year, seven days in a week or 60 minutes in an hour? Why 12 months in a year, seven days in a week or 60 minutes in an hour? I Royal Museums Greenwich. (n.d.). Retrieved October 4, 2022, from https://www.rmg.co.uk/stories/topics/why-12-months-year-seven-days-week-or-60-minutes-hour

Why are computer errors called bugs? bug meaning in computer. CodingHero. (2021, May 1). Retrieved October 5, 2022, from https://codinghero.ai/why-are-computer-errors-called-bugs/

Why are ivy league schools called "Ivy leagues?". College Raptor Blog. (2022, June 9). Retrieved October 4, 2022, from https://www.collegeraptor.com/find-colleges/articles/questions-answers/ivy-leagues-called-ivy-leagues/

Why are there 24 hours in a day, but 60 minutes in an hour? Science ABC. (2022, July 8). Retrieved October 4, 2022, from https://www.scienceabc.com/eyeopeners/why-are-there-24-hours-in-a-day-and-60-minutes-in-an-hour.html

Why are there 24 Hours in a day? THE IFOD. (2020, April 17). Retrieved October 4, 2022, from https://www.theifod.com/why-are-there-24-hours-in-a-day/

Why are there Interstate Highways in Hawaii? Hawaii Answers. (2014, September 17). Retrieved October 5, 2022, from https://www.hawaiianswers.com/why-are-there-interstate-highways-in-hawaii/

Why can't we control each of our eyes to see different things ... - quora. Quora. (n.d.). Retrieved October 4, 2022, from https://www.quora.com/Why-cant-we-control-each-of-our-eyes-to-see-different-things-simultaneously

Why do beans make you fart? New Health Advisor. (n.d.). Retrieved October 5, 2022, from https://www.newhealthadvisor.org/Why-Do-Beans-Make-You-Fart.html

Why do people shake hands? Why Do People. (2016, May 23). Retrieved October 4, 2022, from https://whydopeople.net/why-do-people-shake-hands

Why do people shake hands? Why Do People. (2016, May 23). Retrieved October 4, 2022, from https://whydopeople.net/why-do-people-shake-hands/

Why do people speak different languages? Culture Online. (2021, March 23). Retrieved October 4, 2022, from https://www.ucl.ac.uk/culture-online/ask-expert/your-questions-answered/why-do-people-speak-different-languages

Why do the british drive on the left? Almanac.com. (n.d.). Retrieved October 5, 2022, from https://www.almanac.com/fact/why-do-the-british-drive-on-the

Why do we blow out birthday candles? Wonderopolis. (n.d.). Retrieved October 4, 2022, from https://wonderopolis.org/wonder/why-do-we-blow-out-birthday-candles

Why do we have two eyes? in addition, why aren't there more than two ... Quora. (n.d.). Retrieved October 4, 2022, from https://www.quora.com/Why-do-we-have-two-eyes-In-addition-why-aren%E2%80%99t-there-more-than-two

Why do we yawn? all causes and best facts of yawning. HearingSol. (2020, April 29). Retrieved October 5, 2022, from https://www.hearingsol.com/articles/why-do-we-yawn-causes-and-facts/

Why does the sun set in the west?? - brainly.in. brainly.in. (n.d.). Retrieved October 4, 2022, from https://brainly.in/question/27748567

Why is it that boogers and tears taste salty? ^_^. Answerbag. (n.d.). Retrieved October 5, 2022, from https://www.answerbag.com/q_view/480059

Why is urination referred to as 'number 1' and defecation as ... - quora. Quora. (n.d.). Retrieved October 5, 2022, from https://www.quora.com/Why-is-urination-referred-to-as-number-1-and-defecation-as-number-2-How-did-these-specific-euphemisms-originate

wikiHow. (2022, July 28). How to urinate outside discreetly: 14 steps (with pictures). wikiHow. Retrieved October 5, 2022, from https://www.wikihow.com/Urinate-Outside-Discreetly

wikiHow. (2022, May 27). 4 ways to fix a keyboard that has the wrong characters. wikiHow. Retrieved October 5, 2022, from https://www.wikihow.com/Fix-a-Keyboard-That-Has-the-Wrong-Characters

Wikimedia Foundation. (2022, July 18). New Year. Wikipedia. Retrieved October 4, 2022, from https://en.wikipedia.org/wiki/New_Year

Wikimedia Foundation. (2022, June 22). Veterans Day. Wikipedia. Retrieved October 4, 2022, from https://en.wikipedia.org/wiki/Veterans_Day

Wikimedia Foundation. (2022, October 3). Punxsutawney Phil. Wikipedia. Retrieved October 4, 2022, from https://en.wikipedia.org/wiki/Punxsutawney_Phil

Wikimedia Foundation. (2022, October 4). The flintstones. Wikipedia. Retrieved October 5, 2022, from https://en.wikipedia.org/wiki/The_Flintstones

Wikimedia Foundation. (2022, September 1). Caboose. Wikipedia. Retrieved October 5, 2022, from https://en.wikipedia.org/wiki/Caboose

Wikimedia Foundation. (2022, September 24). Earth day. Wikipedia. Retrieved October 4, 2022, from https://en.wikipedia.org/wiki/Earth_Day

Wikimedia Foundation. (2022, September 25). Groundhog day. Wikipedia. Retrieved October 4, 2022, from https://en.wikipedia.org/wiki/Groundhog_Day

Wikimedia Foundation. (2022, September 27). Gregorian calendar. Wikipedia. Retrieved October 4, 2022, from https://en.wikipedia.org/wiki/Gregorian_calendar

Wikimedia Foundation. (2022, September 27). Valentine's Day. Wikipedia. Retrieved October 4, 2022, from https://en.wikipedia.org/wiki/Valentine's_Day

Wikimedia Foundation. (2022, September 5). Comb. Wikipedia. Retrieved October 5, 2022, from https://en.wikipedia.org/wiki/Comb

Wikimedia Foundation. (2022, September 9). History of AC power plugs and sockets. Wikipedia. Retrieved October 5, 2022, from https://en.wikipedia.org/wiki/History_of_AC_power_plugs_and_sockets

Winner, M. M. (2022, January 24). Why do people throw rice at weddings? Brides. Retrieved October 4, 2022, from https://www.brides.com/why-do-people-throw-rice-at-weddings-5073735

Wisitech. (2021, December 23). Know all about all hallows' eve or Halloween: Halloween prayer request. The Salvation Garden. Retrieved October 4, 2022, from https://www.thesalvationgarden.org/know-all-about-all-hallows-eve-or-halloween/

Yadav, P., & Yadav, C. (2022, September 23). Difference between interstate and highway [updated 2022]. Ask Any Difference. Retrieved October 5, 2022, from https://askanydifference.com/difference-between-interstate-and-highway/#

Zielinski, L. (2020, February 24). What happens if the Groundhog sees his shadow? Metro US. Retrieved October 4, 2022, from https://www.metro.us/what-happens-if-the-groundhog-sees-his-shadow/

Čirjak, A. (2020, June 16). Why is a day 24 hours long? WorldAtlas. Retrieved October 4, 2022, from https://www.worldatlas.com/articles/why-is-a-day-24-hours-long.html